INSPIRING TALKS

by

J. VERNON JACOBS

for

Superintendents

Youth Leaders

Teachers

Speakers

STANDARD PUBLISHING
Cincinnati, Ohio
2961

PREFACE

The popularity of *Sixty Short Talks for Superintendents and Youth Leaders* has brought a request for another, similar volume. *Inspiring Talks* has been prepared to fulfill this request as well as the needs of church groups and youth organizations.

The talks may be used not only in worship services and evening youth meetings, but for summer camps, vacation Bible school devotionals, Y.M.C.A. and Y.W.C.A. organizations, chapel services, scout groups, and other youth gatherings.

The talks deal with common problems, and an effort has been made to provide satisfactory answers to them. Most of the talks contain enough points that ministers can develop them into full-length sermons if they desire.

J. VERNON JACOBS
Phoenix, Arizona

Table of Contents

Clean out the Attic

Have you ever planned a move to a new city? If so, you will probably remember that one of the biggest tasks connected with moving was sorting all of your belongings, packing the useful ones and getting rid of those items you did not need or want. No doubt you went through everything you had, carefully evaluating each thing. When you went up into the attic you probably found there things that had been accumulating for years, things that were really nothing more than a fire hazard—old dusty trunks, faded letters, broken furniture, souvenirs, toys, and worn-out clothing. At one time these things had meant a lot to you, but now they were only cluttering up the place. Certainly they would not fit in with the new home to which you were going!

The new year is at hand. You are taking a journey into a brand-new land where you have never lived before. Surely you do not want it cluttered up with a lot of things that are useless, or even detrimental. So go up to the attic and see what is there. Get rid of the rubbish that has collected.

If *envy* is there, do not carry it over into this bright new year just beginning, for it will paralyze mind and body. You may be richly endowed with talents, and yet become a "nobody" simply because you spend your time envying another instead of developing your talents. In Old Testament times Saul was the first king of Israel. He brought much unhappiness and misery upon himself and his family because of his envy of David and the fear that David would take his place. Instead of doing his very best in the situation, he spent his time and effort in trying to destroy David. Get rid of fear this year. Don't let it ruin your life. Resolve that you will use the talents God has given you.

Do you have any *grudges* up in the attic? They are bad, and spoil your happiness completely. Benedict Arnold was a brilliant soldier during the American Revolutionary War, but he became bitter because he was bypassed for promotion. Others went ahead of him. His bitterness led to the betrayal of his country and a wretched life in the land of his enemies. Do you recall the brilliant Aaron Burr? He blamed Alexander Hamilton for his defeat in a presidential race. His hatred led to his killing Hamilton in a duel. No one respected him very much after that. His last years were filled with misery. Certainly you will not want to carry grudges over into the new year.

What about *bad habits?* Are they cluttering up your attic? Get rid of them! At first they may appear harmless, even very pleasant; but later they will enslave you, and then destroy you. I once saw a big, strong man trying to break the habit of smoking cigarettes. What a struggle he had to wage! Smoking had given him a chronic cough, bad nerves, impaired digestion, and an irregular heart. But the habit had enslaved him. Maybe this is not your bad habit, but if you do have one, get rid of it before it becomes more difficult to break. Do not keep it until it has mastered you.

Do you have *evil desires?* Do you sometimes want to wrong someone or see a certain classmate fail? Do you secretly hope that some boy who has a classy hot rod will wreck it? Do you hope that the star player on the basketball team will get sick so you can take his place? Do you long to do a certain thing that you know is wrong and sinful? Clear the attic of evil desires this year. Get rid of your fear, grudges, and bad habits, and this will indeed be a happy new year for you!

What Are You Worth?

At the death of Roger Ascham, brilliant English scholar, and tutor to Queen Elizabeth I, the queen exclaimed, "I would rather have cast ten thousand pounds into the sea than to have lost Ascham!" This was worth about $50,000, but in buying power would have been worth a lot more. What are you worth to someone else?

When the war between the states broke out, the North made an effort to enlist the services of Robert E. Lee, who was a graduate of West Point. But he could not think of helping in an invasion of his native state and the South. General Scott insisted that Lee was worth fifty thousand men in battle. Are you as valuable as an entire group of people?

Adalbert, of Prague, sought in vain to convert the Bohemians to Christianity. Then he sought to convert the Prussians. But he was murdered in A.D. 997. When this happened, Boleslas, duke of Poland, bought Adalbert's body for its weight in gold and brought it back. Adalbert now became more influential than he had been while he lived. The Bohemians, remembering his good works, now opened up the city of Prague to the church. Are you living such a life that your good works will be remembered after your death?

At the beginning of each year, places of business take inventories, and books for the past year are closed. These business establishments make an effort not only to determine the profits of the past year but their net worth. As you start out on this new year, take inventory of your life. What are you worth, not in dollars and cents, but in value to the world? Let's consider your worth in three categories.

1. *What do you know?* Are you just a parrot, speaking to others only what you have been taught and what you have read in books? Or do you have some original ideas that you have thought of all by yourself? Have you learned how to

think clearly and how to do research and investigation on your own? What specific contribution do you hope to make to the welfare of the world? Will the world be better off, or worse, because you have lived?

What do you think about the really important things of life? What do you know about God, the meaning of life, God's plan for you? What are the true values of life, the things worth living for, and the things worth dying for? What do you know about the plan of salvation, the spiritual life, and life after death? Consider all these questions carefully to learn what you are worth in knowledge.

2. *What do you believe?* The person who does not believe anything in particular is like a ship drifting at sea, with no one to guide it, and no port ahead. The men and women who have done the most for the world have been people of great convictions and high ideals. They have had Christian principles to guide them, and their accomplishments have been the result of working toward definite goals. Could you sit down today and make a list of great convictions by which your life will be guided? Draw up such a set of principles and use them during the years ahead. Then you will arrive somewhere because you will know where you are going. True Christian principles will start you on the way to greatness.

3. *What are you willing to pay for success?* Are you willing to work hard? There was once a boy who lived in a poverty-stricken home. He received only a month's schooling each year and had to be on his own from the age of ten. But he managed to read a thousand books, and became a legislator before he was thirty. Did you ever hear of Henry Wilson? He was one of our vice-presidents. He worked hard for his success.

Make yourself valuable this new year—valuable to yourself, your family, your friends, your country, and especially to God and His kingdom.

What Do Others See in You?

What kind of face do you have? Do you consider it handsome, plain, pretty, "cute," distinguished, or perhaps even ugly? Do you resemble someone in your family—a sister or brother, one of your parents, or a grandparent? Perhaps you don't think about your face very much. Or maybe you think about it too much because of a too-prominent feature or a flaw of some kind. Physical features are interesting, aren't they?

Sometimes, however, a person with a beautiful face can look ugly. On the other hand, a person with a plain face sometimes appears to be very pretty. Why is this true? We might say it is because of the personalities of the individuals. All of us, in addition to our physical facial features, have personality traits that help to tell others what kind of persons we are. These traits are more important than the color of our eyes, the shape of our noses, or the size of our mouths. Qualities that can make a person appear to be ugly are selfishness, jealousy, anger, deceitfulness, hate, vanity, etc. Do people see any of these in you? If a person lives with any of these bad qualities long enough, people will soon know he is selfish or deceitful or vain.

There are also qualities that can make the person with even the plainest face appear to be beautiful: kindness, generosity, love, honesty, humility, goodness, patience. I hope these are the qualities people see in you. I hope your life shows that you are living close to God. Have you ever seen an individual change from the practice of hate to love, the practice of selfishness to generosity, from the practice of deceitfulness to honesty? God and Jesus Christ can cause such a change. Let God help you to write a message of goodness and beauty with your life! Surrender yourself wholly to God's will to be formed and framed as He wishes. Then others will see Jesus in you.

Thy Speech Betrayeth Thee

Peter was warming himself at the fire in the courtyard of the high priest during the trial of Jesus, when someone said, "Surely thou also art one of them; for thy speech bewrayeth [betrayeth] thee." Peter had a Galilean accent and it served to identify him as one of the followers of Jesus.

Whenever you are ill and visit a doctor, one of the first things he says is, "Let me see your tongue." By the appearance of your tongue the doctor can often determine what is wrong inside of you. The tongue, as it speaks, also tells what is wrong inside of you. It reveals what kind of person you are—what you think, feel, wish, and plan. "The mouth of a righteous man is a well of life," said Solomon of old, "but violence covereth the mouth of the wicked." Jesus said, "Of the abundance of the heart the mouth speaketh."

If a man is ignorant, just let him talk a few minutes, and everyone will know it. Someone has jokingly said, "I am always perplexed as to whether to refuse to speak up and let everyone think I am ignorant, or to open my mouth and let them be sure of it." It is amazing today how few people use good English, and resort to modern slang. Yet jobs are lost for just that reason. In many professional fields, it is almost impossible to advance to successful positions without almost perfect usage of the English language.

The sound of your voice can also betray you. Make a tape recording of your conversation with someone for a half hour, then play it back. You will find out just how you sound to other people. It will not only reveal the quality of your voice, but it will disclose whether it is hard and cruel, insolent or boastful, deceitful, hateful, or filled with pride. You may be shocked, but if it inspires you to improve, it will be worthwhile.

Your humor may also betray you, if you have been in the habit of telling off-color stories. Certainly what you think funny is an indication of the kind of person you are. There is a place for humor in life, but be sure it is the wholesome kind that gives a lift without leaving behind something harmful to the souls of those who hear. A group of military men were gathered when an officer entered and said, "I've just heard the best story. There are no ladies present, are there?" "No," replied the general, "but there are gentlemen." The story was not told. If you have a talent for making people laugh, it is a fine gift. But be sure your humor never embarrasses or shames anyone.

Your speech will betray you if you are tellng lies. Khrushchev made himself ridiculous at the summit conference in Paris when he said, "As God is my witness, my hands are clean and my soul is pure." As a communist he is an avowed atheist, responsible for the deaths of many. Not many people are able to tell lies and make people believe them. As one woman said, "I have to listen to a man only a few minutes to know whether he is a phony or not."

The tongue is a troublesome member, writes James, and anyone who is able to control it can control the whole body. "Therewith bless we God, even the Father; and therewith curse we men, which are made after the similitude of God" (James 3:9).

If the tongue can betray you and let the world know your bad qualities, it can also reveal good things about you. It can tell of your kindness, sympathy, and love. It can witness to your faith in Jesus Christ and to your loyalty to the church, God's kingdom. What does your speech tell about you?

Do You Want to Be a Leader?

(Youth Sunday)

Many young people aspire to be leaders. They envy those who have places of responsibility. Perhaps they would like to be elected to class offices; or maybe they dream about being a recreation leader so they could plan and conduct clever parties. Many would like to be chosen to sing solos, or be asked to take leading parts in plays. Some young people who do not attain desired positions may feel that those who do attain such positions do so because they have "pull," are from wealthy or socially prominent homes, or are the favorites of those who do the choosing or appointing. Most of the time this is not true at all. People are chosen because they have leadership ability, and because their friends have confidence in them. No one wants to ruin the work of an organization by selecting incompetent leaders. No one wishes to spoil a program or play by giving parts to favorites who are not capable. There are real reasons some young people are chosen in preference to others for places of leadership and responsibility. What does it take to become one of the chosen ones?

1. *Ability to plan and think*. Have you ever belonged to a club or organization that had poorly planned meetings? If so, you probably noticed that the attendance was poor and interest was fading. The leader of the group evidently did not take time to think about the meetings in advance. No goal was set to accomplish, nor was there any real purpose in the meetings because of the leader's lack of preparation and planning. Unless a leader can think and plan logically, he is not really a leader, for no one will follow him.

2. *Willingness to work*. No one ever does a brilliant job without putting in many hours of drudgery. The halfback on the football team does not win his place by being a friend to the coach. He puts in long hours of practice, takes many

hurts and bruises, and maintains a rigid discipline. The coach is not going to risk losing games just so he can use some favorite student. He is out to win, and will use any man who comes through with the right performance on the field.

The president of the student body is more than someone who is well-liked by the students. He is nominated and elected because they believe he has real ability, and will represent their interests when problems arise. He may seem like a glamorous figure as he stands on the platform, but he is going to put in many hours of work with committees and faculty, while the other students are out having fun.

3. *Good character.* No organization wants a leader or president who is incapable, undependable, or who has low ideals. People want a representative of whom they can be proud. If you have lost out in a class or group election, or some other desirable position, there is a reason. You ought to find out what it is. Knowing the reason and making the proper adjustment and improvement may lead to the attainment of your goal.

4. *Ability to get along with people.* No matter how talented a person may be, if he cannot get along with people, he will be a failure. He must not try to drive his associates, but lead them. He must not humiliate them when they make mistakes, but patiently help them to do better. He must praise them when they do well and encourage them when they fall short.

5. *Prayerful attitude.* A good leader knows that he cannot do everything by himself. He needs not only the help of his associates, but he needs God's help. In everything he does, he should depend on God to help him. Keeping in close touch with God through prayer is a must for any real leader. Any good work that a leader can do will be much better and more worthwhile if he seeks God's help.

Do you want to be a leader? Examine yourself to see if you have what it takes. Then strive to improve yourself in the five points we have discussed.

Rainbows in the Storm

After the great flood, Noah, his wife, his sons, and their wives came from the ark to begin civilization all over again. God promised them that whenever a rainbow appeared in the sky it would be a reminder that the earth would never again be destroyed by water. We like the rainbow. It is a thing of beauty, and it assures us that God's promises are real. We can trust Him. There are storms in life that come to us. When they come, God's promises are as rainbows in the sky. They help to cheer and encourage us when days are dark. They give us assurance that the storms will pass.

Have you lost your job? Why did you lose it? Perhaps it was unjust of your employer to discharge you. But on the other hand, perhaps it was your fault. Were you ill-prepared and inefficient in your job? Were you wasteful, dishonest, or disagreeable? Perhaps you didn't take God with you into your job. Remember, God has promised in His Word, "Seek ye first the kingdom of God, and his righteousness; and all these things shall be added unto you." (See Matthew 6:33.) Your main job is the work in God's kingdom.

Have you lost your girl friend or boy friend? Why? Perhaps you were too selfish and demanding. Maybe you were rude, inconsiderate, unkind. Jesus can help you to overcome these bad traits. However, it may have been that your girl friend or boy friend was not right for you. Paul warns, "Be not unequally yoked together with unbelievers" (2 Corinthians 6:14). Whatever the problem, let God guide you in the matter.

Whether your problem be poor health, financial worries, the loss of a loved one, or some other storm of life, you can trust God to see you through it. Perhaps your problems will not be solved in the way you had hoped, but God will do what is best for you. Remember always that "all things work together for good to them that love God" (Romans 8:28).

Do You Ring the Bell?

Bells are delightful things. They were used for many purposes during the past. In some places they were used to call the people to assemblies in the village square; in other places they were used to spread an alarm, warning of the approach of an enemy or the starting of a fire. In times of victory, bells were rung to express the joy of the people and their praise to God for the help He had given. Train bells were used to warn of danger; sleigh bells brought delight to people who were out to enjoy the snow. Anyone who has read Edgar Allan Poe's poem, "The Bells," will remember how graphically he has described the different types of bells and how they stirred the emotions of the people.

In ancient times, when people were very superstitious, it was believed that the ringing of bells would scare the devil away. Then there was the old school bell. It used to boom its deep tones across the town, warning pupils to hurry and get ready, or they would be late for school. Church buildings had bells also. Children always seemed to envy the man who rang the bell to call people to church. When there was a funeral, the bell in the church building tolled mournfully. Weddings were made happier with the ringing of the church bell. Something very precious was lost when churches discontinued using bells.

Today we often hear the expression, "He really rang the bell that time." This means that someone did something exceptionally well, or accomplished something unusual. Do *you* really ring the bell? You do not if you are a do-nothing, if you are lazy, or not thorough in anything you attempt. Do you want it to be said of you, "He really rang the bell"? How can this be accomplished? Let us see if we can think of some ways.

Perhaps you would like to "ring the bell" as a speaker. If

17

so, you are going to have to work hard to learn to speak in an interesting manner so that people will want to listen to you. You will have to be willing to talk about ideas that are new and different as well as those that are old and already accepted. You will have to know not only how to deliver a speech well, but how to write a good speech. Are you willing to put in the time and effort necessary to "ring the bell" as a public speaker?

If you are in charge of a program, and you want people to say, "She really rang the bell that time," you will have to show some originality and a lot of planning. Develop an appropriate theme in a new way, using new talent, different decorations, clever invitations, etc. Avoid monotony! Variations in your programs will do more to promote good attendance than anything else.

Do you have a particular talent with which you want to "ring the bell"? Whether you are a singer, pianist, excellent personal worker, typist, or good cook, you can work hard to develop your talent for your group, church, and especially for God. Most important, be sure you "ring the bell" as an individual. Make your life pure and good. Live close to God so that your life will "ring out" for Him and His Son, Jesus. People will look up to you and admire you for the Christian you are. *Do You Ring the Bell?*

Be a "Somebody"

Do you want to become famous? There have been thousands of people in the past who have done so. There will be countless thousands in the future. You have no doubt studied enough about famous people to know that fame does not come by wishing or by trying to "pull strings." A person cannot buy or bribe his way to true greatness, nor does fame come simply by having a famous person in your family. On the other hand, a person does not have to be rich or handsome to become famous. Let me give you some examples of poor boys who became truly great men in spite of their poverty.

Michael Faraday was a poor boy, apprenticed to a bookbinder, when he became ambitious to do something great. He became a great chemist and physicist. Henry Clay was called "the millboy of the slashes." He never went beyond the three R's in formal schooling. But he taught himself and advanced to a place of high honor in our country. Abraham Lincoln had little classroom study, but he walked great distances to borrow books to read and study. For years people thought he was a nobody, but millions wept for him when he died. James A. Garfield drove mules that pulled a canal boat. He worked his way through school. But he attained the White House. Booker T. Washington, a slave boy, worked in a coal mine and studied in night school. He worked very hard and overcame great obstacles to become the founder and president of the famous Tuskegee Institute.

What are the elements of greatness that a person must have if he is to become famous?

1. *He must be a prepared person.* No man ever became great because he was ignorant, but there have been many ignorant people who could have become great if they had been willing to spend long years learning, working, and preparing for greatness. "A lot of people have been lucky," you may say.

That is true but you must remember that luck is simply opportunity knocking on the door of a prepared person. The important thing is to be ready for the important task when it comes your way.

2. *He must be a doer.* No "do-nothing" ever became great, even though he may have inherited a million dollars. There are several millionaires in the country, but how many do you recognize as being great? Aren't they the few who became great by doing something good for humanity. There is an interesting book in which twenty-two millionaires tell "How I Made a Million Dollars." These men were doers! They began with pennies, but made them grow into fortunes. Greatness comes by long hours of work, deep thought, courage, and useful service.

3. *He must be a person of high ideals.* It is true that some of the famous men of history have been selfish, scheming individuals who came to power through a sea of blood. When their lives are examined, we wonder who set up the standards that allowed them to be listed among the great. In contrast to these, we like to think of men who placed their trust in God to help them become great.

4. *He must be humble.* The truly great person is one who does not think of himself as great. He has become aware of the fact that all of his knowledge is but a drop in the ocean of divine wisdom, and that the service he has rendered is pitifully small in comparison with the needs of the world. He is not haughty and cold, but approachable; he is not cruel, but kind; he is not a boaster, but one who accepts his work as a responsibility, and keeps self in the background.

It is good to keep in mind that not all the great people of this life are to be found in the pages of history. But their names have been written in God's "book of life." Remember, Jesus said, "Whosoever exalteth himself shall be abased; and he that humbleth himself shall be exalted."

Is Your Heart Right?

Every year a month is set aside in which we are asked to learn things about the heart. We are also asked to support research in trying to find ways of stopping death due to heart disease. The heart is a very amazing organ. Day and night it works without ceasing for many years. It rests for only a fraction of a second between beats. Repairs have to be made while it is in motion. People who wish to live long must learn how to take very good care of their hearts.

More important than the physical heart, however, is the spiritual heart, or the soul. Is your "heart" right toward God? You should keep this question before you always. With the heart we love God; with the heart we believe "unto righteousness" (Romans 10:9, 10). When the Ethiopian said to Philip, "Here is water; what doth hinder me to be baptized?" Philip answered, "If thou believest with all thine heart, thou mayest" (Acts 8:36, 37). Jesus said, "For out of the abundance of the heart the mouth speaketh" (Matthew 12:34).

When something is physically wrong with the heart, various warning signals occur: palpitations, skipping of beats, slow or rapid pulse, or pain. Warning signals also occur when the heart is not right spiritually. Are you stubborn, determined to have your own way, regardless of what God wants? Does evil appeal to you more than good? Do you have to be urged to attend church services, not finding delight in doing so? These are all warning signals, indicating "spiritual heart trouble." We should heed these warnings.

We urge you to turn to Jesus, the great Physician, who will forgive your sins and heal your spiritual diseases if you obey Him. Death often comes suddenly and unannounced. Don't say, "It won't happen to me." It can happen to you. But if your heart is in God's keeping, you need not worry about the future.

Can We Get Rid of Guilt?

People were made to be good. So, when they live wickedly there comes a sense of guilt that can make them utterly wretched. They become restless, nervous, ill at ease. Their lives are without joy because of their accusing consciences. They wish heartily they could get rid of their guilt, but do not know how to do it.

During the middle ages there were groups of people known as flagellants who often marched through the streets, scourging themselves or cutting themselves with knives until the blood flowed. They hoped that by suffering they would find peace, but it failed to come. Today there are some people who believe that if they do a little more good than bad, the bad will be canceled out. They will have no more guilt. This is a mistaken notion. Sin carries a penalty that cannot be blotted out by any amount of good one might do, nor any amount of money one might pay. Many people try to silence their consciences by giving large amounts of money to charity or other worthy causes, but guilt cannot be eliminated so easily.

When David sinned, he learned what unhappiness it brought. In the Fifty-first Psalm he cried out, "Have mercy upon me, O God . . . blot out my transgressions. Wash me throughly from mine iniquity, and cleanse me from my sin. For I acknowledge my transgressions: and my sin is ever before me. . . . Create in me a clean heart, O God; and renew a right spirit within me. Cast me not away from thy presence; and take not thy holy spirit from me. Restore unto me the joy of thy salvation; . . . Then will I teach transgressors thy ways; and sinners shall be converted unto thee."

God doesn't want to keep people wretched because of guilty feelings. He has given us consciences so that we can be prodded into righting the wrongs we have done, and turning our hearts to Him. He has no delight in punishing people, and whatever chastisement He may send us is for our own good. He realizes that people make mistakes sometimes, but He isn't going to hold these mistakes against them forever unless they force Him to through continued disobedience. He is interested in their becoming better people and doing good works for Him in this world. He is more concerned about the future than the past, and is eager that we make ready for life with Him.

How can you get rid of guilt and have joy come back into your life? If you are not a Christian, you need to receive Christ as your Saviour. You need to be obedient to Him in Christian baptism. "Repent, and be baptized every one of you in the name of Jesus Christ for the remission of sins" (Acts 2:38).

If you are already a Christian and make a mistake, you will need to repent and to ask forgiveness. "If we confess our sins, he is faithful and just to forgive us our sins, and to cleanse us from all unrighteousness" (1 John 1:9). When we are forgiven of our sins, guilt will go from us.

Whose Side Are You on?

Children are not in this world very long until they become aware of the fact that there are opposing forces in life, and that they must be on one of at least two sides. Whether they are playing cowboys and Indians or sandlot baseball, they must choose sides. In high school it may be the matter of a debate team, or the campaign to select class officers. In adult life a person selects one of several political parties, chooses between Christianity and opposing forces such as communism, and decides whether to serve God or Satan. Whatever it concerns, sooner or later a person is asked, "Whose side are you on?"

In Old Testament times, after the Israelites had entered the land of Canaan and conquered the pagan tribes that occupied it, some of the people began to be attracted to the fantastic rites of heathenism. Joshua, their leader, called them together and challenged them. "Choose you this day whom ye will serve," he demanded, "but as for me and my house, we will serve the Lord." (See Joshua 24:15.)

Jesus is calling upon every one of us to make a decision to-day. We cannot be on both sides; we must be either for Him or against Him. In Laodicea there were those who wanted to be saved, but they did not want to carry on Christ's work. To them He said, "I would thou wert cold or hot. So then because thou art lukewarm, and neither cold nor hot, I will spue thee out of my mouth" (Revelation 3:15, 16).

Let us see what the devil offers you. He will let you do absolutely as you please in this life. You may lie to your friends, cheat your employer and the government, get as drunk as you wish, disgrace your parents, become a hoodlum, take to dope, live a degraded life, kill your enemies, and do other terrible things. He doesn't tell you, of course, that you will lose your self-respect, cause grief or harm to others, suffer guilt and shame, lose your friends, cut short your life, and lose your soul. Those things he would not want you to think about. He wants you to see just the glamour and tinsel of sin as it is in the beginning, not the ugly, hideous thing it is at the close. You need not go very far to see the degradation that sin causes. Go to the prisons and study the people who are there. See how the devil treats those who go all out for him.

In contrast to this, Jesus offers you true and lasting happiness, self-respect, the satisfaction that comes with worthy service, and everlasting life. Which of the two ways of life would a wise man choose? Which would a fool choose? The answer you give to this greatest question in life is going to prove whether you are a wise person or a fool.

"Let me wait awhile," you may say. "Let me choose later." Many people have waited until sin has so hardened their hearts they couldn't change. Others have succeeded in changing, but deeply regretted their wasted years. Still others have waited, only to have their lives taken from them before choosing to serve Jesus.

Today we are inviting you to make the great decision, and choose Christ for your Saviour. This is more important than selecting the kind of career you will follow. It is even more important than choosing a husband or wife. The decision to accept Christ puts you on God's side, and gives you a heavenly helper who will assist you in doing right. It brings you a gift that cannot be bought with money—everlasting life. Do you want it? Choose to follow Christ today!

Salvation

It is confusing to people, as they visit different churches and hear various appeals made, to know how to be saved. There are conflicting voices and many different ways pointed out. Who is right? How can anyone be absolutely sure how to attain salvation?

First of all, let us see what will *not* save us. Membership in a congregation does not save us. Having our names in a church roll book isn't any guarantee that we will go to heaven. There are a lot of names on church rolls that are not in the Lamb's book of life. The Bible tells us that the Lord adds us to His church.

Goodness does not save us, for no one has ever been good enough except Christ himself. No matter how upright and moral a person is, he is lost if he has not accepted Christ as his Saviour. Of course a saved person strives always to be good, but goodness alone saves no one.

Giving of our money does not save us. No amount of money will buy our way into heaven. Giving is a necessary part of living the Christian life, but it alone cannot save us.

There are two parties to the covenant that comprises salvation. The first is Christ. He made atonement for our sins on the cross, and provides salvation for us. It is a gift, but it is a conditional gift, and He has decided the terms. Christ has done His part, and if we do ours, then we are saved people. What is our part? What does He ask of us?

1. *Faith in Jesus as the Son of God* (Acts 16:31). A person must believe beyond all doubts that Jesus is more than a good man or a wise teacher. He must believe that Jesus is deity, the Son of God, and equal with God.

2. *Repentance of sins.* Repentance is more than being sorry for sins committed in the past. It is a changing of direction—turning from a life of sin without Christ to one of striving for

sinlessness with Christ. Jesus said, "Except ye repent, ye shall all likewise perish" (Luke 13:3).

3. *Confession of faith in Christ.* Jesus wants us to acknowledge Him before men. This is similar to a soldier's taking his oath of allegiance, or two people taking the wedding vow. It is establishing a relationship with God. Paul wrote to the church at Rome and to all who would read His letter, "If thou shalt confess with thy mouth the Lord Jesus, and shalt believe in thine heart that God hath raised him from the dead, thou shalt be saved" (Romans 10:9).

4. *Baptism into Christ.* Each person who believes in Christ is commanded to be baptized. (Read Acts 2:38; Romans 6:3-6; 1 Peter 3:21.)

5. *Continued faithfulness to Christ.* Christ asks us to be faithful to Him throughout our lives. Jesus said, "Be thou faithful unto death, and I will give thee a crown of life" (Revelation 2:10).

Above all we need to remember that it is God's grace that saves us through our obedient faith. Eternal life is for those who have enough faith in God to accept His Son and be obedient to Him. Won't you become a saved person?

The Lord's Supper

(This may be used as a chalk talk. Draw a cross at the beginning of the talk. Then, as the topics are discussed, write "Memorial" at the top of the cross, "Communion" at the left, "Pledge" at the right, and "Spiritual Food" beneath the cross.)

The Lord's Supper was instituted by Jesus. Early Christians met regularly to observe it. It still has a central place in the worship of the church, but if it is to have real value, its meaning ought to be clearly discerned.

1. The Lord's Supper is a *memorial*. Everyone wants to be remembered. Young people sign their autographs in school yearbooks and exchange photographs so their classmates will remember them. Sometimes wealthy men or women erect buildings bearing their names so they will be rememberd. Jesus also wants to be remembered. But He did not build a statue of himself, or a pyramid, or a building of some kind that only a few people would ever be able to see. He wanted a memorial that could be set up in every country and in every age. When He had finished eating the Passover supper with His disciples in the upper room, He took some bread, gave thanks for it, and broke it, saying, "This is my body which is given for you: this do in remembrance of me" (Luke 22:19). In the same manner He gave them grape juice, representing His shed blood. And so through all the succeeding centuries, as His followers come together on the first day of the week, they have remembered with gratitude the sacrifice Jesus made for them.

2. The Lord's Supper is a *communion*. It is a time when we meditate on what Christ did for us in providing salvation through His blood. We review our lives during the week that has passed and become conscious of our shortcomings. We become increasingly glad that Christ made atonement for us, and that we can have forgiveness because of what He did for us

on the cross. We utter a silent prayer of thanks, letting Him know of all our appreciation. We wait for Him to speak to us. Good thoughts flow into our minds. We feel cleaner and stronger because we have honored and remembered Him as He asked us to do.

3. During the Lord's Supper we make a *pledge*. As we think of Christ and all He did for the world, we realize that just being thankful is not enough. We want to be better than we have ever been before. We want to accomplish more for Him and His kingdom. We realize that there is a world program that He asked us to carry on, and that it can never be realized unless we get busy and do our part. We want to see His message carried to the ends of the earth, and we want His cause to be victorious. So, we think on these things with heads bowed and eyes closed, and we make a pledge to Him. Christ did not ask us to make such a pledge. It is the spontaneous response of the heart to Christ's love and sacrifice. In our pledge we promise to be more faithful in attendance, in consecration, and in giving. We are going to show our loyalty in serving Christ more diligently. We resolve that we are going to break our bad habits and that we are going to be more kind and loving. We are determined to control our tongues, and to say no when we are faced with temptations.

4. The Lord's Supper is *spiritual food*. The experience of remembering, showing gratitude, soul-searching, pledging, and cleansing does for the soul what food does for the body. It brings a renewal of spiritual life, fortifies the will, cleanses the conscience, and deepens the devotion for God. It opens the heart and mind for an inflow of the divine Spirit, and helps us to become more like the One who loved us and gave himself for us.

Remember these four meanings when you partake of the Lord's Supper. You will be a much richer Christian, and the Lord's Supper will be more valuable to you.

The Tomb With a Broken Seal

(Easter)

Many people had seen Jesus die on the cross. They had been terrified by the darkening of the sun, and the earthquake that accompanied it. Jesus was placed in a rock-hewn tomb with a great stone at the entrance, and the seal of Caesar placed on the stone. Roman soldiers were left to guard the tomb.

Then came the third day and Jesus' resurrection. Soon Jesus was showing himself alive to His disciples and others. In one instance He appeared to more than five hundred people in a group. He had brought others back to life; now He had been raised by the power of God and was living proof of His ability to conquer death.

Fifty days after Jesus' resurrection the church was founded. The message of that first day was one of the fulfillment of prophecy, of atonement, salvation, and the assurance of life beyond the grave. If the seal on Christ's tomb had not been broken, the church would have been laughed out of existence. The multitude gathered for Pentecost simply would have said, "His body is still in the tomb; the seal is unbroken. The story of Jesus' resurrection is only in your imagination." But the multitude could not say that, for the empty tomb was there, and many people had seen the risen Christ.

Men have always hoped for a life beyond death. In ancient Ur of Chaldea, tombs have been unearthed showing that men believed in another life. Accompanying their bodies were all those things people might need on their journeys into the other world. Evidence of similar beliefs has been found in Egypt, where bodies were embalmed. In Greece, the philosophers talked of immortality long before the days of Jesus. In America, Indians placed with the dead a horse, dog, and food.

Finally, at Jesus' resurrection, life after death became a

proved fact. On the Day of Pentecost, three thousand people, who were in a position to know the facts, acknowledged their faith in the resurrection of Jesus. Christians, today, acknowledge their faith in this historical fact.

Paul, in speaking before King Agrippa, said, "Why should it be thought a thing incredible with you, that God should raise the dead?" (Acts 26:8). Is it any harder to bring back to life a body that once contained the spirit than to have created a man in the first place? Is there any sense in living at all, if about the time we have some understanding of life, we should be cut off from it entirely?

We can be grateful, however, that this isn't the case. Death is not the end, but the beginning. It is not the going out into unconscious oblivion, but a coming into eternity. This life is but the preparatory stage of an existence that is to go on and on forever. What in former centuries may have been only a hope became a reality when Christ demonstrated that men can live and die, and then live again.

"There is a natural body," said Paul, "and there is a spiritual body. . . . And as we have borne the image of the earthy, we shall also bear the image of the heavenly" (1 Corinthians 15:44, 49). "Flesh and blood cannot inherit the kingdom of God," Paul also asserted. Even those who are living on the earth when Christ comes again will be changed in the twinkling of an eye so that they will no longer have physical, earth-bound bodies, but spirtual bodies, fitted for life in spiritual realms. We merely lay aside our old, worn-out bodies, which are no longer capable of serving the soul, and enter into brand-new ones. Thus we shall be able to enter into the activities of the heavenly home that is being prepared for us. Let us be glad on this resurrection day that Christ was raised from the dead to live forevermore. Let us give thanks to God and praise His name for the wonderful promise of life everlasting.

No Shadowboxer

Many people today do not take seriously the reality of the devil. To them he is just a symbol of evil, or, at the most, a sinister influence. These people are much like the little girl who had learned the truth about Santa Claus. When her Sunday-school class had a lesson on the devil, she spoke up and said, "Aw, there isn't any devil; it's just our daddy."

Unless we understand and know the devil for what he really is, we cannot hope to overcome evil. If we think of him as just a symbol or idea, we shall be like shadowboxers, merely beating the air or a hazy shadow.

The devil, or Satan, is a personality. Paul insisted that this evil personality must be overcome. Satan is out to destroy us because of his hatred for God. We are his targets. Every day he tries in various ways to win us to his side. The closer we draw to God, the harder Satan works. The more we read God's Word and pray, the more Satan tries to fill us with his lies. Just as we are Satan's targets, so should he be our target. Always we must be on the alert for his sly tricks and attractive temptations. He will try to win us by any means he can—even by using our friends and families. Who do you think prompts a friend to say, "Oh, it won't hurt you to miss church this one time"? It is Satan. Who tries to make worldly pleasures look more attractive than serving God? Satan. Who advances the theory that experiencing sin will help us to resist it? Satan.

While it is true that the closer you live to God the harder Satan will work on you, it is also true that the nearer you are to God the better able you will be to fight and conquer Satan. Jesus used the Word of God to help Him resist Satan's temptations. We, too, can battle against Satan with the Word of God; but we must be very familiar with it before we can use it as an effective weapon.

So you see, we are not shadowboxers when it comes to our

fight with Satan. We are fighting against a real, living, evil personality—one who is out to win over us at all costs. Let us be the victors, the champions along with Christ over Satan. We can be sure of this: no matter how hard Satan works, no matter how many people he wins to his side, Jesus will overcome him. Do you want to be on the winning side against Satan?

Hidden Worlds

Isn't the world beautiful? We glory in the beauty of its mountains, lakes, rivers, trees, and flowers. We are grateful to God because certain things in the world are so dependable. We can be sure that the sun will rise and set, the seasons come and go, and that the crops will grow. We live in the midst of wonders that we cannot understand, and bow in reverence before the Creator, who is so great, wise, and good.

In addition to our visible world, all about us are hidden worlds that we do not see. They are, nevertheless, very real. First, there are the worlds beneath the earth which are inhabited by insects, worms, and other forms of life. In these worlds there is the same struggle for existence that we have. Their lives are regulated by a God-given law that we call instinct, and they follow without fail the same pattern, generation after generation.

There is also a world in a drop of water. If you have studied biology, you will remember how amazed you were when you put a drop of water under a microscope and found it alive with countless protozoa that were swimming about contentedly, seeking food, or engaged in combat. Most of the microscopic beings in water are harmless. Our city water systems bring us pure water. But sometimes wells and springs contain bacteria that may cause sickness and even death. The water may be cold and sweet, but it holds an invisible world of dangerous, microscopic creatures.

At the bottom of the ocean there is another invisible world. It is inhabited by various kinds of odd-looking creatures, many of which have never seen the light of the sun. Indeed, we never knew they existed until scientists of recent years invented instruments by which they can be detected. These too are God's creatures, and they live according to His laws. From the beginning of time they have existed, apparently unaware that there is any other world but the one in which they live.

Let us turn our attention toward outer space where we see thousands of stars. Beyond these are millions of worlds which the telescopes have brought near. They are great burning worlds, one of which is at least seven-billion miles in circumference, and thousands of light years away from the earth. Whether or not these worlds are inhabited is a matter of speculation. But we can be sure that God has them there for a purpose.

Think of the sandy deserts. Many times we think of them as barren places where nothing can grow. But scientists have proved this is not so. With powerful microscopes they have discovered evidence of tiny flowers of wonderful beauty.

There is another invisible world—it is better than all the others, and the most important place of all. It is the place to which we want to go after death. We cannot see it now, even as we cannot see the stars when the sun is shining. Not until darkness falls do the stars shine out in all their beauty. So it is with us. When we shed our worn-out bodies, we shall enter into new, spiritual ones. If we have been obedient servants of Christ, we shall see the glory of the wonderful world, now hidden from us, where we shall spend eternity. Jesus Christ is there now, preparing it for us. We too must be preparing, looking forward to the time we can be there with Him—the time when the most wonderful world of all will be our home for eternity.

What Happens When We Die?

What happens to us when we die? Everyone sooner or later considers this question and people have different ideas. Some people believe that man is only an animal without a soul, and that when he dies he merely ceases to exist. This belief is opposed to all Biblical teaching. It would allow people to live any way they pleased. They could do great evil, injure others, and live on the level of animals, never having to give account to God. There are others who believe that the soul goes into a deep sleep at death and will not awaken until the end of the world. It is true that Jesus spoke of death as a sleep because it resembles sleep. He wanted people to understand that the soul of a "dead" person still lives, just as we live even while sleeping. Only the body of a "dead" person sleeps while his soul or spirit continues to be aware of his surroundings.

Death is a separation of our souls from our old, worn-out bodies. These bodies, when they die, are no longer capable of sustaining the spirit. They will be exchanged for new, spiritual bodies, fitted for eternal life. Our present bodies are suitable only for a short while on this earth. They have great limitations. They need food, rest, and exercise. Even when a physical body receives the right amount of these things it "wears out" in a comparatively short time. We learn from Paul that even those who are still living on earth at the time Christ returns will have their bodies immediately changed. With their new spiritual bodies they will ascend to meet Him in the air (1 Thessalonians 4:17).

This present body is subject to age, pain, disease, and death. When Gulliver, of the famous fairy tale, came to the land of the Luggnaggians in his travels, he found that some of them were born to be immortal. *How wonderful,* he thought, *for people not to have to worry about death.* But he found that these people were not happy. At eighty they had all the natural weaknesses that come with old age, but they could not die. After two hundred years had passed, the language of the country had changed so much that these people couldn't even carry on a conversation. Yet they could not die. What a terrible fate!

Our new bodies will not be subject to sickness, pain, and death (Revelation 21:4). "Flesh and blood cannot inherit the kingdom of God," said Paul (1 Corinthians 15:50). "As we have borne the image of the earthy, we shall also bear the image of the heavenly" (1 Corinthians 15:49).

At death we close our eyes to this world, to open them up in a spiritual world. According to Jesus' story of the rich man and Lazarus, angels were present to carry righteous Lazarus to paradise, the waiting place of the righteous dead. The rich man, on the other hand, was already suffering in the place prepared for the wicked who die, because of the evil life he had lived on earth.

Paul at one time was privileged to look into paradise, and he saw wonderful things that he was not allowed to tell (2 Corinthians 12:1-4). That experience was an inspiration to him as long as he lived. In the transfiguration, Moses and Elijah, dead for hundreds of years, appeared to talk with Jesus. They had not died as beasts and ceased to exist. They weren't unconscious in the grave. They hadn't merely faded off into oblivion. They were real, live people, awaiting the final judgment.

If you are a Christian, you need not fear death. It is not a jump into darkness, but a passing into realms of light, for God dwells in light. If you have been faithful to Christ you need not fear the judgment, for it will be a time of reward. You will enter heaven to experience the fullness of life that Jesus came to proclaim, and toward which you have worked. For all eternity you will live in the presence of God and Christ.

Foolish Promises

In the days when judges ruled the people of Israel, there lived a young man named Samson. He fell in love with a Philistine girl, and tried to nag his parents into making arrangements for a marriage. It was the custom for the parents to make such arrangements in those days. These Jewish parents begged Samson to turn his attention to some of the girls in Israel, but he would not listen. He kept after them until they finally promised to make the proper negotiations. It was a foolish promise, made against their better judgment and against the law of Jehovah. It was a promise that led to much sorrow for Samson and the people of Israel.

In the days of the Jewish patriarchs there lived twin boys, Jacob and Esau. Jacob was an ambitious young fellow, aspiring to be the leader of the tribe; but he was the younger of the twins, and the leadership rightfully belonged to his brother. Esau, on the other hand, was happy-go-lucky, more interested in hunting than anything else. One day Esau came back from the hunt very hungry. Jacob was cooking some tasty stew, and it smelled so good that Esau wanted some. "Sell me your birthright and I will give you some," Jacob said. Just then the leadership of the tribe meant very little to Esau. "What good is the birthright when I am about to starve?" he asked. He promised his birthright to Jacob. He sold it for a mess of pottage. Years later he was sorry for his foolish promise and bad bargain, wishing heartily that he had never done the deed.

In New Testament times, Herod Antipas gave a big banquet. He invited noted people to attend. As part of the program the daughter of Herodias danced. Her dancing so pleased Herod that he promised, "Whatsoever thou shalt ask of me, I will give it thee, unto the half of my kingdom." Now the girl's mother, Herodias, hated John the Baptist, who had been thrown into prison. So she instructed the girl to ask for the head of John the Baptist as a reward. When Herod heard this request, he was very sorry, for he looked upon John as a prophet and knew that John's death would cause sorrow among some of his people. But all about him were his guests, waiting to see if he would keep his promise. So Herod ordered John to be executed.

Down through the ages people have made foolish promises. They are still doing it today. What are some of the foolish promises young people make? Sometimes parents decide upon a certain occupation they wish their son to follow. They use all their persuasive powers to get him to agree to take up that occupation. The boy knows he has no interest in or talent for that vocation, but to keep peace in the family he agrees to do as his parents wish. What a foolish promise to make! No parent has a right to force a child into a career he dislikes. Don't make such a promise. You will have to either break it or be unhappy with it all your life.

Sometimes a young person promises to marry someone he or she does not really love. Yet, because the engagement has been made, the person feels he must go through with the marriage. Of course such a foolish promise never should have been made, but it is better to call off a wedding even minutes before the ceremony than to endure a life of unhappiness and misery.

Occasionally there is a parent who makes his children promise not to marry as long as the parent lives. This is a bad request. Requesting such a promise is motivated by selfishness, not love. Don't make such a foolish promise.

Foolish promises should not be made in the first place. But if you have made one, it is better to break it than to cause wrongdoing and heartbreak by keeping it. Good promises are fine, but unwise or careless ones can lead you to ruin. Make your promises carefully.

Understanding Your Mother

(Mother's Day)

We often hear young people complain, "My parents just don't understand me." Did you ever stop to think that perhaps young people don't try to understand their parents? Understanding is a "two-way street." At this time when we are paying special tribute to our mothers, let us see if we can understand them a little better. How does your mother feel about you? What does she expect from you?

1. Your mother is interested in your welfare. She has seen your growth through the years. She glories in your talents as she sees them coming to light. She wants you to make a fine success of your life. She has guarded your health, made sure you ate the right food, and provided for your needs for many years.

2. Your mother wants you to be a person of fine character and integrity. She is eager for you to become a student of the Bible, to know God and His plan for salvation. She wants you to be loyal follower of the Master. If you fulfill these wishes, she will feel that her life has been worthwhile.

3. Your mother expects you to obey her as long as you live in your parents' home and accept their food, shelter and other provisions. She expects you to respect her opinions even if you do not agree with them. She wants to advise and guide you and help you to solve your problems. She has learned much, and wants to share her experiences with you.

4. Your mother wants your love and affection. She has given you her love for many years. Surely she deserves your love in return.

Try to understand your mother just as she is trying to understand you. You will be surprised and pleased with the happy relationship you and your mother will share.

Can You Pass the Exam?

It is just about time for final examinations in the schools and colleges of the country, and many young people are cramming for these important tests. There is much at stake. If a young person fails a course, all of the semester's work has been for nothing, as far as school credit is concerned. Your record for the semester is just what you have made it. How glad you will be when examinations are over, and you have received that precious degree or high school diploma. Then you won't have to worry any more about taking examinations. Or will you? When you finish school and enter into the business and social world, you will find that every day is examination day. You had better know the right answers!

When the world was very young, Adam and Eve were placed in the garden of Eden. They were given work to do. They were to care for the beautiful garden. God permitted them to eat of the fruit from all the trees in the garden but one. This one was forbidden. But along came Satan and tempted them to eat from the forbidden tree. He told them things that were not true, making them think that God was unfair to them. So Eve ate of the fruit and gave some to Adam. That evening, when God came to talk with Adam and Eve they were hiding. They knew they had done wrong. They had not passed the test. Are you doing any better than Adam and Eve?

Joseph, as a young man in the house of Potiphar, an army officer, had served his master so well that he was promoted to be in charge of all Potiphar's possessions. One day when Potiphar was away on military business, his wife sought to seduce Joseph, but he refused. "Why, my master has trusted me with everything he has," said Joseph. "How can I do this great wickedness, and sin against God?" Joseph passed his test.

In the year 586 B.C., the city of Jerusalem was destroyed by the Babylonians, and the Hebrew people were carried into captivity. Among them were four young men, one of whom was Daniel. These four were chosen for special training. They were to eat at the king's table, partake of his rich food and strong drink. These four boys had evidently been reared in devout Jewish homes. They knew the dangers of strong drink and rich foods. They asked to be served only simple food to eat and water to drink. The steward was shocked and afraid of what the king might say. "Put us on a ten-day test, and then compare us with the other young men," urged Daniel. Finally the steward consented. At the end of the ten days the four young men looked better and their minds were keener than all of the others being trained. So they continued with their simple food. They made a better record than the wise men and the magicians of the king. They passed their exam because they chose the right way, God's way.

You are going to have many temptations to face, many exams to pass. What kind of answers will you give to such temptations? Perhaps you will face strong temptations when you go away to college, or to the big city to work. Perhaps you will go into the armed forces. A young person's character is truly tested when he is away from home. It is then that the parents' teaching proves to be either a success or a failure. It is then that a person shows whether he is a true Christian or one in name only. Think ahead. Have your answers ready —the right ones—if you want to pass your examinations in life.

The Boy Who Never Grew up

Some years ago Sir J. M. Barrie wrote a play called "Peter Pan." It was about a boy who overheard his parents discussing what they were going to make of him when he grew up. Right then he decided to run away to the fairies and never grow up.

Do you know that there are many teen-agers who seem to have made part of that decision. Perhaps most of them do not run away from home, but they do not grow up. They can't get along with their parents; and when they do not get their way, they put on a scene, making everyone thoroughly unhappy. They do not conduct themselves as young ladies and gentlemen, but as little spoiled children. You know, it is possible for a person to be six feet tall, seventeen years old, and still be just a "big baby." No one can tell him anything, and he resents any suggestions made to him. He balks at being told or reminded what to do, but will not do it without being told. He feels that anyone who tries to help him is trying to run his life and therefore he will accept no help. He would rather do a poor job by himself than admit he needs help in order to do a good job.

When is a person grown up? When he begins to behave as a grown-up and mature person. An adult welcomes knowledge and helpful suggestions. He is guided by reason rather than by his emotions. An adult develops self-control and an even temper. An adult is willing to forgive, and doesn't spoil his life by holding grudges. An adult is forgetful of self because he thinks in terms of helping others. And yet he is always striving for self-improvement. Are you grown up or are you like Peter Pan, the boy who never grew up? We hope that all of you will try hard to be growing young people, working for maturity in every phase of your lives.

Watch Your Patches

One day the disciples of John came to Jesus with a question. The question is not important to us right now, but the answer Jesus gave is significant: "No man putteth a piece of new cloth unto an old garment, for that which is put in to fill it up taketh from the garment, and the rent is made worse" (Matthew 9:16).

Probably none of you is wearing a patched garment today, though there is certainly nothing disgraceful about it if you are. But you know what would happen if a new piece of cloth were sewed to old material, especially if the new piece of cloth were not pre-shrunk. When the garment was washed, the new piece would shrink and tear away from the old, leaving a hole in the clothing worse than the original. The lesson for us to remember is this: "Don't put together things that do not harmonize." Watch your patches, or you will be worse off than before.

1. *Knowledge and ignorance do not harmonize.* Suppose that a handsome boy who had quit high school before graduating persuaded a college-educated girl to marry him. The young man's world is limited by the factory where he works and the television set which he watches every night. He does not have any interest in improving himself. He has no desire to go with his wife to places of culture and meetings that she enjoys. The two young people actually live in two different worlds. Soon they drift apart because they have no common interests to help them live harmoniously.

2. *Poverty and riches do not harmonize.* Now suppose that a poor man marries a rich girl. "You can love a rich girl as much as a poor girl," he tells himself. But the young man does not have much earning power himself, and soon he finds that things are not going so well. His wife has been accustomed to a standard of living that he is not able to sustain.

44

She offers to provide money from her own funds, but it hurts his pride and he becomes resentful. He feels that other people look down on him. Little by little the husband and wife grow apart and find their happiness diminishing.

3. *Good and evil do not harmonize.* A girl becomes infatuated with an attractive young man who drinks, gambles, and has a selfish disposition. She imagines that she can change him. After the couple is married, the girl soon sees her mistake. The drink habit continues to grow; home life becomes wretched. His gambling keeps them in poverty, and his disposition kills the love she had for him. Only unhappy years lie ahead of her, for happiness stems from harmony in dispositions, habits, ideals, and conduct. As static drowns out sweet music, evil ruins the lives of those who think it can live side by side with good.

4. *Faith in God and unbelief do not harmonize.* "All that matters is that we love each other," says a Christian young man who has married an unbelieving girl. But that is not all that matters. When he wants to go to church, she insists on taking sight-seeing trips. He wants to read his Bible regularly, but she has only scorn for it. He wants to go to prayer meeting; she prefers playing cards with the neighbors. He wants to start each day with devotions; she ridicules the idea. What is likely to be the outcome of such a combination? Paul warned, "Be ye not unequally yoked together with unbelievers: for what fellowship hath righteousness with unrighteousness?" (2 Corinthians 6:14).

As you begin to consider what kind of lifetime mate you want, be sure to "watch your patches." Choose someone who will harmonize with you and with God's plan for your life.

Tales From Distant Lands

Today I would like to tell you some brief stories about people in distant times and faraway places.

William Carey was a missionary to India. Imagine how horrified he must have been to see Indian parents sacrificing their children at the great annual festival at Gunga Sangor. With God's help he taught the people that this was wrong. Soon this terrible practice was stopped. Later he was able to stop the natives from burning widows on the funeral pyres of their husbands.

Robert Moffat, a missionary to Africa, once stopped overnight at the home of a rich South African farmer. The farmer asked him to conduct a worship service. When Mr. Moffat insisted that the servants also participate, the man was shocked. "Hottentots!" he roared. "Are you come to preach to Hottentots? Go to the mountains and preach to the baboons. Or, if you like, I'll fetch my dogs, and you may preach to them."

In those days the white farmers did not believe that the Hottentots had souls or could be taught. Mr. Moffat then read the story of the Syrophenician woman, and took for his text Matthew 15:27: "Truth, Lord: yet the dogs eat of the crumbs which fall from their masters' table." In a little while the man's heart was touched, and he called the Hottentots, who heard the gospel for the first time.

In many heathen lands people wear charms that they believe will protect them from evil spirits. One day Dr. A. L. Shelton, missionary to Tibet, noticed a man wearing a charm, and talked to him about it. The man was sure of its protective power. Dr. Shelton challenged, "Suppose you stand out there and let me shoot at you just once. If I don't hit you, I will buy that charm at your own price." The man refused, as Dr. Shelton knew he would. "We'll try it on a goat," said the doctor, who had one he intended to butcher. The charm was placed on the goat, and the doctor, being an excellent shot, hit the charm in the center, killing the goat. The man was amazed, and his faith in heathen charms was broken.

Samuel Crowther was an eleven-year-old Negro boy. He was captured by Arab slave traders and put on board a slave ship. A British vessel stopped it and liberated the prisoners. After being taken to Liberia, he was put in a mission school, then sent to England. Finally he came back to his homeland to be a missionary. There he found his mother, whom he had not seen for twenty-five years, and he had the joy of leading her and many others to Christ.

Andoniram Judson, missionary to Burma, was put in prison by the natives. His wife had to pay the jailer to get to see him. Once she sent him a message baked in a cake; once she put a letter in the mouth of a coffee pot. A copy of the Bible that he had been translating she sewed into a pillow; he read it by day and slept on it by night. Even though he remained a prisoner for two years, his faith was kept steadfast and strong.

When on the way to India as a missionary, Alexander Duff was shipwrecked. He and the passengers swam to a nearby island. Everything on board the ship was thought to be lost. But one day a package containing Mr. Duff's Bible and hymnbook floated to shore. These were the only things saved from the wreck—the things he needed most for his work.

Children's Day had its beginning in 1880, when three children heard Dr. J. H. Garrison praying that missionaries might be sent to distant lands. Wanting to help, they gave him $1.13 from their savings bank to help with the work. Dr. Garrison took the money to a missionary convention and told the story. Hearts were touched and people were stirred to do great things for missions. Won't you help as those children did to send our missionaries into all the world to preach the gospel?

Do You Have "Eyes That See Not"?

In 1961 the newspapers carried a story about Christine Blanche la Barraque, who died at the age of ninety-two. Born in a tiny French village near the Pyrenees, she lost her eyesight at the age of two, and lived in darkness for nine-tenths of a century. You might suppose that, like countless other blind people, she went through life dependent upon others, but this was not the case. She was brought to America when she was twelve years old, and she became the first blind woman to graduate from the University of California. Two years later she was the first blind woman to be admitted to the practice of law in that state. She was interested in singing, so she went to the Boston Conservatory of Music, and then to Italy to study voice. Later she became a teacher of voice. So pleasant was she, and so well did she adjust herself, that it seemed hard for people to realize that she was blind.

The classic example, of course, is that of Helen Keller, who became both blind and deaf at the age of nineteen months. She not only learned to speak, but she graduated with honors from Radcliffe College at the age of twenty-four. She has written books, given lectures, and has even made a motion picture having to do with her life story. She has traveled the world over, bringing messages of courage and hope to people who are similarly handicapped, and she has set up an endowment fund for the American Foundation for the Blind. She has been honored by the great in many lands, but she never has lost the humility that is characteristic of her.

"Blind Tom" Bethune, a Negro slave boy, was born blind in 1950. He never saw a piano nor a note of music, but he just seemed to have music in his soul, and someone taught him how to play. It soon became evident that he was a musical prodigy, because once having heard a piece played, he could immediately reproduce it accurately on the piano. His fame soon spread, and he was taken all over the country to present piano concerts.

Another "Blind Tom" was Thomas P. Gore, who lost his sight as a child. At twenty-two he graduated from college with a law degree, and went on to become a United States senator, serving twenty years.

William H. Prescott, a famous American historian, lost an eye while he and his college classmates had a "biscuit battle." His other eye became practically useless. But he had set his heart on being an historian, and he went ahead in spite of this great handicap. During the latter half of his life, he had people read to him from various sources as he gathered material for the many volumes that he wrote.

I am wondering what you would have done if you had been in the place of any of these persons. Would you have said, "There is no use for me to try to do anything"? Would you have been a burden on your parents all your life? Would you have depended on others to support you, received your living from some government agency, and made no contribution to the world?

More important, however, what are you doing with the two good eyes you do have? Are you willing to study hard to prepare yourself for something worthwhile? If you are out of school, and it is too late for you to attend full time, are you willing to read books and magazines, attend night classes, enroll in leadership-training schools, and do other things that will make it possible for you to serve in a larger way than you are doing at present?

One day Jesus was talking with His disciples, and they just didn't get His point at all. He rebuked them because they had "eyes that see not and ears that hear not." Are you going along through life with eyes that do not see, and ears that do not hear?

Are You Following the Pattern?

When the Israelites came to Mount Sinai on their way to the Promised Land, God gave them the law, and also ordered them to build a tabernacle as a place of worship. Calling Moses up on the mountain, He gave him specific directions as to how the structure was to be built. God urged Moses to see that the pattern given him was followed exactly.

People who live in the south or southwest find the heat of the summer very oppressive. Many of them put up cabins in the mountains or along the seashore so they can enjoy the cool breezes. But they don't just order a pile of lumber and start nailing it together. Even small, one-room cabins call for blueprints, with specific directions and instructions as to how the cabins are to be built. If the directions aren't followed, the cabin is likely to be unstable and unsightly.

A father proudly said concerning his daughter, "She's making her own clothes now." The girl had learned to follow a pattern. It's fun to select a pattern and material and then see a garment take form as the pattern is followed. Of course you might try cutting and sewing the material without a pattern. If you did, it would probably end in ruin, unless you were an experienced seamstress. No, you want every piece to be cut exactly and put together perfectly, and this requires a pattern.

Sometimes a boy who wants a hot rod goes to a car dump to salvage enough pieces to make one. He doesn't throw the pieces together in just any fashion (although some older people may suspect as much). There is a place for every piece, and if he does not put the pieces together correctly, the car will probably fall apart.

God has given us directions for His church in the book of Acts and in the epistles. If we follow those directions we will have a New Testament church. If we digress, as many are doing today, it will not be the kind of church that was set up in the first century. It will not be the kind of church that Jesus wanted.

If you are wise you will follow God's plan. If a certain practice was a part of the first-century church, begun by the apostles, then the practice ought to be followed today and not changed. When God gave directions in the past, He told His people not to turn to the right hand or the left. In Revelation Christ warns us, "If any man shall add unto these things, God shall add unto him the plagues that are written in this book: and if any man shall take away from the words of the book of this prophecy, God shall take away his part out of the book of life." (See Revelation 22:18, 19.)

Some day make a list of things that present-day churches are not observing as the early Christians did. Today we're hearing a lot about Christian unity. That is good, but it will not come until the churches return to the Scriptural plan for Christ's church. In other words, they are going to have to follow God's pattern, putting all the pieces together in the right way. Then the original church will be restored in all its glory, and Christ's prayer for unity will be realized.

The Songs We Sing

Someone has said, "Let me write the songs of a nation, and I care not who makes the laws." This person believed that songs have a tremendous impact and effect on people, and so they do. We like some songs simply because they are fun to sing and provide an emotional release. Other songs represent certain moods, such as happiness, romance, depression, or sympathy. Some songs have definite teaching values. Since songs have rhythm and rhyme they are easily learned and remembered.

Songs cheer us up when we are tired or unhappy. A bus was making its way across the treeless plains of the Texas panhandle one day. The passengers were tired, and the bus was filled with smoke. Suddenly from the back there came children's voices singing, "Jesus Loves Me." It was like a fresh breeze blowing through the bus over the weary, travel-worn people.

Hymns are especially precious songs because they help to inspire us to worship God, obey His Word, and resist temptations. They encourage us when we feel depressed. They may even be instrumental in bringing someone to Christ for the first time. Many years ago Billy Sunday and a group of ball players came out of a saloon and sat down on the curb. Across the street a mission band began to play hymns, some of which Billy had sung as a boy. His heart was touched, and, arising, he announced, "Boys, I'm through." Eventually he became one of the great evangelists in America.

Too few of us really learn Christian hymns. Perhaps we can hum the tunes, but we don't know the words, much less understand their meaning. Songs have helped men under many adverse conditions. Songs are a precious treasure that may be ours for the asking. Study and know the Christian hymns. Sing them to the praise and glory of God.

What Is Your Temperature?

It is the "good old summertime." We watch the mercury rise in the thermometer and see the weather become a topic of daily discussion. In some parts of the country people are uncomfortable when the register reaches eighty, but in parts of the southwest the people are so used to hot weather that even one hundred degree readings do not bother them. Summertime is a wonderful time of the year. The warm temperatures permit us to be out-of-doors, where we can really enjoy the beauty of God's world.

Body temperatures are even more important to us than the temperature that surrounds us. Most people have an average temperature of 98.6 degrees. If your temperature drops very low, you probably feel exhausted and run down. If it rises a degree or two, you are running a fever, which indicates that the body has some kind of infection that needs the attention of a doctor.

The temperatures of animals are interesting. Warm-blooded animals such as dogs, cats, and rabbits have higher average temperatures than human beings. The temperatures of cold-blooded animals—turtles, snakes, etc.—vary according to the outside temperature.

We could go on and on talking about temperatures and thermometers. We could discuss candy thermometers, meat thermometers, and even temperature gauges for a baby's bath. But our chief concern right now is with spiritual temperatures.

One Sunday a woman left a church building exclaiming, "This is the coldest church I have ever seen." No one had welcomed her or had even bothered to speak to her. How could the people in that church love God very much when they weren't even concerned about other people? Unless a church is friendly, warm, and hospitable, it cannot grow. Not many souls will be won to Christ in such a cold church. The low temperature of a "cold" church will eventually lead to its death.

Christ hated something even worse than a cold church: a lukewarm church. We want the temperature of most things we drink to be either cold or hot. When they are lukewarm they are often very sickening. This was how a lukewarm church affected Jesus. He told the church at Laodicea, "Because thou art lukewarm, . . . I will spue thee out of my mouth" (Revelation 3:16). What is a lukewarm church? It is one whose members are self-satisfied. They see no need to do any more work than they are doing. Perhaps they speak to visitors on Sunday, but they are not interested enough to call on them during the week. They say they love God, but fail to show it.

Jesus wants the spiritual temperature of a Christian to be high. He wants the church to be on fire for Him. Christians should radiate with warmth toward other people. They should be so stirred with love for God's work that self-satisfaction will never set in. They should be fervent in their study of God's Word and in their prayers.

What kind of church do you attend? Is it cold, lukewarm, or hot? What are you doing to help it be on fire for God? The spiritual temperature of a church depends on its individual members. What does your spiritual thermometer register?

Who Wants to Stay Young?

Who wants to stay young? Apparently no one does. "Only one more year until I can go to school," cries Billy in glee. "I'll be glad when I'm older." Janie, who is eight, says, "I'll be glad when I'm old enough to be a girl scout." Big brother, who is in high school, says, "I just can't wait until I get into college." Great big brother, who is in college, says, "One more year, and I can get married." Father, who works in an office says, "In just a few more years I can retire."

Older folks would like to *look* young, so they buy lotions for the skin, take mineral baths, and purchase drugs and vitamins, hoping to put off the day when wrinkles and gray hairs will come. Yet, they don't want to *be* young, for youth is associated with ignorance, insecurity, embarrassment, and lack of skill. Sometimes they *act* young in an effort to impress someone or some group of people. However, this usually gives the impression that they are foolish, and most older people realize this.

So, you see, everyone really wants to grow up, and that is the way God intended for it to be. There is a joy in developing one's talents and learning new things. There is an even greater joy in using our talents and knowledge, especially if we use them for God. No matter what age a person may be, there are pleasant goals just ahead for which to strive, and when he has reached them, he finds that there are now more challenging ones that beckon him on. It is this challenge that makes life interesting and good, full of anticipation, hope, and excitement.

As you grow older, take Christ along with you. Have heaven as your primary goal. If you do these things, your life will be full and rich, no matter what your age. Then, after this life, you will dwell forever, never aging, with God the Father and Jesus Christ.

What Do You Do When You're Scared?

Have you ever been really scared—not just slightly afraid, but really frightened? If you haven't been, you will be, sooner or later, and it will not be a pleasant experience. Your fright may come from a threatened or actual loss of job, money, reputation, health, or life. It may be a moment when your whole future hangs in the balance, and the decision you make will affect your very life and even your soul. It is a dreadful thing to face a crisis and not know what to do. What do people usually do when they are scared?

1. Some people are so *paralyzed* with fear that they don't do anything. That makes them victims of circumstances. The roar of the lion and the scream of the tiger are intended to do just that—paralyze the victim so that it cannot move. Man, with a more highly developed nervous system, has the power to think quickly. He is not nearly as helpless as the animals that depend on instinct. People can usually make split-second decisions that help them in emergencies. Develop your ability to make decisions so fear will not paralyze you.

2. Some peoople will *run,* instead of being frozen in their tracks. Joe didn't believe in ghosts, and so he agreed to sleep one night in a haunted house. About midnight he awakened and saw a ghost standing right by his bed. Out the door he went, running like a frightened deer, the ghost following. Over hill and dale they went until Joe could go no farther. He stopped to lean on a fence. The ghost caught up with him and also leaned on the fence. "Quite a little run we had," said the ghost who turned out to be one of Joe's friends who had played a trick on Joe. "Yes, Sir, and as soon as I get my breath, we're going to have another," replied Joe.

Sometimes it is a good thing to run when scared—run from danger, temptation, and sin. Other times running is cowardly. We need to learn when to run from something frightening and when to stand still and face up to it, ready to fight if necessary.

3. Some people will *lie*. Simon Peter was waiting in the courtyard while Jesus was being tried before the high priest. He was recognized by a young woman there, but he denied that he was one of the followers of Christ. A little later a man pointed him out as one of Christ's disciples, and again he denied it. Still later another person insisted that he was one of them because he was a Galilean. By now Peter was thoroughly frightened. He feared that he might be put to death, so again he denied it, and tried to back up his false statement by cursing and swearing. Peter brought only sin and shame upon himself. Conscience stricken, he went out and wept bitterly after Jesus looked at him. Lying may get you out of a tight place temporarily, but it gets you into a worse place permanently, for no liars are going to enter the gates of heaven. If you have followed the practice of lying in the past, repent and ask God's forgiveness at once. Otherwise, you have no hope of everlasting life.

4. Some people *pray* when they are afraid. When good King Hezekiah found his nation of Judah being invaded by the Assyrian army, he was afraid. He had good reason to be, for the Assyrians had taken city after city. The Assyrian ruler, in his own royal records, said, "Hezekiah himself, like a bird in a cage, I shut up in Jerusalem, his royal city." He sent his general to demand the surrender of Jerusalem, but Hezekiah refused to surrender. Then the Assyrian king sent a letter to Hezekiah. "Have the gods of the other nations delivered them?" he demanded. "Do you think Jehovah is going to deliver you?" Hezekiah took the letter to the temple and prayed. God answered his prayer. That night most of the Assyrians camped outside the city walls were killed, and only a remnant lived to return to their homeland.

When you are afraid or faced with a crisis, pray to God. He will help you to overcome fear and solve your problems.

Hold That Tiger!

During vacation time, when traveling in the West, you may see some tiny bear cubs along the roadside and be tempted to take them home with you. Or, you may find baby kittens of the bobcat or mountain lion, and feel that they will make good pets for the family. It would be dangerous to touch one of them, for one little cry might bring the ferocious mother upon you. She would claw you to pieces in an effort to save her young.

Nevertheless, some people do bring back such pets. They are as cute as can be while young, but when they grow up, they become a problem. Perhaps they do become accustomed to living around people, and even tiger kittens brought from the jungles seem to adjust themselves. But they still have in them their wild nature, which may break forth at any time. A man who has worked with all kinds of wild animals said one day, "You can train animals, but you can't tame them." That is why you hear so often of the grown ones reverting to type, and injuring or killing someone. This often happens in zoos. Without any provocation, the animals suddenly attack their keeper.

There is in man an animal nature, which Paul calls *carnal*. It must be kept constantly in chains, lest it break forth and do evil. It is selfish and will take advantage if it gets a chance; it will roar if enraged and say cutting words; it is impulsive and may injure if not restrained; it is sensual and knows no law but the desires of the body. At first the carnal nature may seem as harmless as a tiger kitten, but unrestrained, it may destroy soul and body. The goal of the Christian is not only to suppress the evil tendencies, but gradually to transform the fleshly nature into the spiritual. As the spiritual nature grows and develops, the carnal recedes more and more until it ceases to be a problem. So, hold that tiger!

Five Ways to Make Friends

There are many ways to make friends, but let us consider five important ones.

1. *Forget yourself and think of others*. If you are sincerely concerned about others more than yourself, you are going to be popular and have friends whether you are good looking or not. Dolly Madison was not a beautiful woman, but she was one of the best-liked first ladies in history, simply because she was always nice to people. It didn't matter to her whether a person was rich or poor, Dolly Madison was ready to do a service. If you continually think about yourself, people will be certain to avoid you. In order to have friends, you must be a real friend.

2. *Ask people's advice*. When you go to someone and say, "I want to ask your advice about a matter," that person is usually pleased. It is a recognition of his wisdom and his willingness to help others. Because you think of him as a friend, he will think of you as a friend also.

3. *Give a compliment* when you can do so honestly. Praise is very precious, and it doesn't cost anything. Be generous with it. Be careful, however, that you do not resort to mere flattery, nor become "gushy," for insincerity is quickly detected. It will cause you to lose friends rather than to win them.

4. *Be co-operative*. Some people won't serve others unless they can have a position of leadership or prominence. This attitude makes a bad impression. Accept the responsibility of a job and do it faithfully; you will win more friends by doing a small job well, than by waiting for an important job just so you can receive notice.

5. *Select your own friends*. If you build your own friendship circle, you will have friends of your own choosing. If you wait for others to come to you first, your choice will be limited. Show kindness to people. Soon they will be your friends.

Samples Are Convincing

Nothing is more convincing than a sample. If you visit one of the supermarkets you often will find uniformed ladies passing out samples of hot dogs, potato chips, crackers, cheese, soft drinks, or ice cream. By mail you may receive samples of soap, perfume, or tooth paste. At your doorstep may be left sample packages of new products. The makers of all these products hope that when you try the product, you will like it and want to buy more. Actual samples of a product are much more convincing than any other kind of advertising could be.

There isn't anything more convincing than a sample in Christianity, either. When someone says, "Those people really live their religion," it is a sign that "those people" have taken their religion seriously. Their sample of Christianity makes an impression that is convincing to others. Paul, in his letter to the Thessalonians complimented them because they had become "ensamples." When he wrote to Timothy, Paul encouraged him to be an example to others.

Harold Begbie, in *Twice Born Men,* tells the story of a character in the slums of London. His name was "Old Born Drunk." He had lived such a life of degradation that mission workers felt there just was not anything that could possibly reach him for Christ. However, from time to time he would slip into the back seat of the mission when services were being held. One night, when the invitation was given to accept Christ, Old Born Drunk shuffled down the aisle. "I want to be like Joe," he said to the one who welcomed him. Who was Joe? He was another drunken character who had made the change some time before. Old Born Drunk had watched Joe and wanted to be like him.

In 1960, Toyohiko Kagawa, the most noted Christian in Japan, passed away. He could have been wealthy all his life, but when he became a Christian his uncle disinherited him.

So he went to work among the most needy people of his city. He shared their lives and brought to them a knowledge of Christ. As he became famous from the great results of his work, he wrote books that brought him a lot of money. He didn't keep the money, however, but used it to help those people in distress. His life has been a challenge and an inspiration to people of all lands. He has been a good example of what Christianity can do for one who is willing to give himself without reservation to the service of the Master.

In Europe there was a young man who was a famous writer, organist, and professor in the University of Strasbourg. He could have continued to live in ease the rest of his life and to enjoy the applause of men. But he had read about the suffering of the natives in the heart of Africa, and he resolved to study medicine and go there as a missionary. He did do that, and for nearly fifty years Dr. Albert Schweitzer has served the ignorant and needy black men in that distant land. He is a fine sample of self-denial and service.

There is a story of a young man who was going up to the lumber camps of the Northwest to find work. "Those fellows are pretty tough characters," said one of his friends, "and it may go hard with you when they find out you are a Christian." Some time passed, and the young man returned. "How did you get along?" someone asked him. "Fine," he replied. "No one ever suspected I was a Christian."

In contrast to that, Paul underwent every kind of persecution. He stood for Christ no matter what the consequences might be. He was beaten, stoned, half starved, and left for dead. He suffered imprisonments and shipwreck, and had to endure countless other sufferings. But he was able to say at the close of his life, "I have kept the faith." Won't you be such an example of Christianity? Samples are convincing!

How Brave Are You?

Suppose someone went to call on a friend, and the one who answered the door said, "I'm sorry, but Bill has the flu, and you had better not come inside." But the caller replied, "Oh, I'm not afraid of the flu. Let me come in and see him anyway." Does *not* being afraid keep one from getting the flu, or tuberculosis, or any other contagious disease? Not at all. People may be susceptible to disease germs whether they are afraid of them or not. Indeed, it is not bravery, but folly, to walk knowingly into danger, for there can be serious consequences.

In certain communities there are religious sects that seek to show their faith by handling serpents during their ceremonies. From time to time they are bitten and they die as a result. Is it bravery to say, "I'm not at all afraid to handle a deadly serpent," or is it folly of the worst kind?

All of us have known young people who have said, "I'm not afraid to associate with wild teen-agers. They won't affect me in the least." Can one listen to bad language, dirty stories, and evil suggestions without being affected by them? No. Years from now they will still be hearing those things as memory recalls them. Is it brave to associate with those who tempt you and dare you to sin? No, it is foolishness. It is no compliment to you that others think you are weak enough to yield. Be brave enough to say no and leave a crowd like that as soon as possible.

"I'm not at all afraid of taking an occasional drink," says a young man. "I know when to stop." But urgings of associates often make a person do what he knows he should not do, and the result may be a fatal accident on the highway, or a moral, physical, and mental breakdown. Alcohol is a habit-forming drug that grows in power and eventually has complete control over its victim.

Curiosity sometimes makes young people do foolish things such as trying dope. Forms of dope are constantly being urged on teen-agers by "pushers" who loiter around the schools. Dope sets up cravings that drive young people to robbery and other terrible crimes, for much money is needed to satisfy the cravings—money that can be attained only by committing crimes for it. If the victims are denied the drugs that their bodies crave, they are driven to even worse extremes. Heroin is one of the drugs that can enslave a person. As yet there is no antidote for it. If you are wise, you will never touch dope under any circumstances. If you are really brave, you will not yield to the temptation to try it just once. You will instead report to the authorities anyone whom you know to be selling it. You will also urge anyone using it to take treatment at once in order to save that person before it is too late. Are you brave enough to do these things?

Long ago Solomon asked these questions: "Can a man take fire in his bosom, and his clothes not be burned? Can one go upon hot coals, and his feet not be burned?" (Proverbs 6:27, 28). No matter how brave you think you are, you cannot associate with sin without suffering from it. As a boy, Augustine associated with a bad crowd. He even pretended that he was worse than they because he didn't want them to laugh at him. By the time he was seventeen, he really was as bad as the others. He lived a life that he would have given a fortune to erase as he looked back on it in later years.

Billy Sunday, as a professional baseball player, knew that he was in the wrong crowd. One day he gave up his old life to live for Christ. It took courage to do that. True bravery is shown not by flirting with sin but by living for Jesus every moment. How brave are you?

How Can We Love God?

One day Jesus was asked the question, "Which is the great commandment in the law?" To this He answered, "Thou shalt love the Lord thy God with all thy heart, and with all thy soul, and with all thy mind" (Matthew 22:36, 37). How can this be done? How can we love God? We cannot see Him, or hear Him speak with an audible voice.

Let us suppose that a young lady moves across the street from where a young man lives. He sees her come and go, and is able to recognize her when he sees her elsewhere. That is *recognition*. Later, he is introduced to her, speaks to her, and occasionally crosses the street to say some word of greeting to her. She is now an *acquaintance*. As time goes on the two young people become better acquainted with each other. Occasionally they go out together on dates. They are now *friends*. Eventually their appreciation for one another grows. They come to have a deep affection and concern for each other. This is *love*.

Now let us see how this may apply to our relationship with God. We see the beauty of the hills, lakes and rivers, the glory of the sunset, and the awe-inspiring universe. We marvel at the millions of kinds of life in the world, especially the human body, so perfectly made, and the mind that is able to think great thoughts and plan great deeds. We realize that all these things did not just happen, that behind all creation there must be a supreme being who is great, wise, and powerful. This is *recognition* of God the Creator.

To find out more about God we turn to the Bible as the only source of revelation concerning Him. We learn about how He brought into existence this world of ours, what His plan was for the people He created, and the promises He made to them. God has now become an *acquaintance*. As time goes on we discover new truths from His Word. We read of Jesus,

God's Son, and the salvation He has provided for us. We realize that He, as well as God, is now a *friend* to us. In gratitude we resolve to accept Jesus because of His sacrifice and commit our lives to Him and His Father in heaven. God is now not merely a friend. He has become our heavenly Father, and we are members of His family. We have established a new relationship, based on mutual *love*.

This new relationship calls for daily association with God. Whereas in the past we only knew *about* Him, now we feel that we know *Him*. We enjoy this fellowship that we have with Him, and, having talked with Him, we sit in silence listening for His voice. We do not hear an audible voice, of course, but He speaks to us through His Word and by His divine providence. We sense His presence and have an increasing certainty that He is real and always with us. His love for us and all that He does for us calls forth a corresponding reaction in our hearts. The love we feel for God and for all of His goodness is not something that flashes down on us from the sky. It is an appreciation that increases as time goes on.

Love that is secret does not do anyone much good. We have to make known our love, and we want to do it if we really love someone. More than that, we want to do nice things for someone we love. We want to give that someone pleasant surprises, help in time of need, sympathy in suffering, and useful service. So it is with God. If we love Him, we will do things for Him. We won't wait until people urge us to accept responsibility in the church, but gladly volunteer. We will not look upon a task as a dull duty, but we will glory in it because we love God and want to serve Him. Jesus said to His disciples one day, "If ye love me, keep my commandments" (John 14: 15). Do you really love God?

How to Face Temptation

There always have been temptations and there always will be. We cannot run away from them, as the old monks tried to do during the middle ages, by fleeing to the desert. Temptations will follow wherever we go. We have to face them, and we ought to know what to do.

1. *Avoid them if you can.* During the days of the old west, a young fellow became a Christian. But he continued to tie his horse up to the hitching post in front of the saloon when he came to town. A friend said to him, "No matter how strong you think you are, let me advise you to change your hitching post." We should not deliberately place ourselves in the way of temptation.

2. *Think ahead and plan.* You know what your weaknesses are, and you ought to decide ahead of time what you will do or say when faced with temptation. Don't wait and be surprised by it, for in your confusion you may make a wrong decision.

3. *Pray.* God has promised to make a way of escape, if you will turn to Him for help. There are many ways in which He can do that, and He will come to your rescue if you depend on Him to do so. You should not walk open-eyed into temptation, however. You have no assurance that God will help you if you do.

4. *Give God time to come to your aid.* Refuse to be rushed into an immediate decision if there is any doubt about whether a matter is right or wrong. Trust God to help you.

Bad thoughts, habits, and desires ought to be replaced with good ones. Be so involved in good activities that you will have no desire or time for wrong ones. Talk with your parents, the minister, and especially God about questionable pleasures. They will help you to resist temptations that could lead you into sin.

Are You Still on the Bottle?

Are you still on the bottle? I do not mean a whisky bottle, nor the bottle containing any other alcoholic beverage. I refer to a milk bottle. In his letter to the Corinthians Paul wrote, "I . . . could not speak unto you as unto spiritual, but . . . as unto babes in Christ. I have fed you with milk, and not with meat: for hitherto ye were not able to bear it, neither yet now are ye able" (1 Corinthians 3:1, 2). Here were people who had been nominal Christians for a number of years, yet they had not grown in the Christian life. They were just like babies who had to be fed milk, when they should have been able to take the strong meat of the gospel.

There are too many people like that in the church today. They have to be taught over and over the very simplest things. They don't know the Bible for they never read it. They cannot quote Scripture passages, for they have never learned them. Surveys throughout the country show that the average church member can repeat only the Ten Commandments, the Twenty-third Psalm, and the model prayer. They learned these things when they were children. They have never grown up spiritually. They still require milk, or the fundamentals of the faith. They are not able to respond to a stronger diet, dealing with the deep, spiritual problems that require wisdom and understanding. If the minister gives a thought-provoking sermon, they may complain that he is "talking over their heads."

The writer of Hebrews said, "When . . . ye ought to be teachers, ye have need that one teach you again which be the first principles of the oracles of God; and are become such as have need of milk, and not of strong meat" (Hebrews 5:12). That is why so many churches have a teacher shortage; their members are still spiritual children, needing to be taught themselves, rather than keen-minded adults, capable of declaring the gospel.

Do not stay on a diet of milk all your life. Begin now to know the Bible, for it is the greatest book in all the world. Make use of the church and public libraries. Borrow some good commentaries and study them with the Bible so that you will be able to understand God's Word better. Read some books dealing with theology so you will know something about the nature of God, His plan for the universe, the work of the Holy Spirit, the plan of salvation, the nature of eternal life, the facts of judgment, and the end of the world. Study books of an inspirational nature which will lift your soul toward God; read practical books that deal with the church and its mission in the world, the meaning of worship, and the responsibilities of stewardship; read books that will help you to see the needs of the world and challenge you to do something about them. Don't go through life half-starved when there are thousands of volumes that can increase your knowledge, develop your character, and give you the courage to live nobly in the midst of a world that knows too little about God and His Son.

Do you find it hard to do right? Grow up spiritually. It may be hard for a child to keep from taking apples from his neighbor's tree, but it is not hard for his father. He has grown up. He has developed self-control.

Do you find it hard to forgive others? Then you are still in need of spiritual growth. Jesus said, "Do not return evil for evil, but good for evil." Do you know someone who treats you unkindly? Be especially kind to that person. Soon he will be treating you with kindness too.

The best part of growing up is the continuing love and fellowship you have with God. The more you grow, the more you will enjoy talking with Him, and receiving guidance from Him; you will be more and more grateful for the daily strength and help He will give you. Lay aside the bottle. Feed yourself with the meat of God's Word!

How to Keep Out of Trouble

We may not know who started that old saying, "Curiosity killed the cat," but we do know that curiosity gets a lot of people into trouble. In the Garden of Eden Adam and Eve had been forbidden to eat the fruit of a certain tree, but the devil tempted them. They disobeyed God and were banished from the garden. Pandora, in the famous legend, permitted her curiosity to get the better of her. She opened a forbidden box, only to wish heartily that she had never done so.

Curiosity in itself is not bad. It is simply the desire to know things. It encourages study, investigation, and research. It leads one to look through the microscope to discover disease germs or the telescope to discover millions of worlds out in space. It leads men to a study of God, the meaning of life, the way of salvation, and what lies beyond the grave. It causes people to want to visit distant lands and to wonder if people live on other worlds. It causes us to speculate as to what life will be like in the world that is to come.

Curiosity, however, must be kept under control. In satisfying her curiosity about the taste of the forbidden fruit, Eve sinned and brought trouble upon herself, her husband, and all generations to come. Pandora's curiosity brought her trouble also. Perhaps you would like to know what whisky, wine, or brandy taste like, and the effect they will have on you. But there are some things it is better never to know. Curb that curiosity if it is bidding you to take forbidden paths—paths that will lead you into sin.

Make your curiosity work for you instead of against you. Channel it into paths of effective service for God. Cultivate a desire to discover God's will for man. If you let your curiosity work for you, you will not need to worry about getting into trouble. You will not be led into paths of sin, but rather into paths of righteousness.

The Door Without a Handle

Can you imagine anyone making a door without a handle? To the surprise of those who look at Holman Hunt's great masterpiece, "The Light of the World," in which Jesus stands knocking at a door, there isn't any handle on the door. But Holman Hunt intended for it to be that way. He wanted to bring out the fact that when Jesus stands before the door of our lives, that door must be opened from within. He never forces himself into the lives of those who do not want Him. He is eager to be a holy guest, but He wants to be an invited guest. Only you can let Him inside. "Behold, I stand at the door, and knock," said Jesus. "If any man hear my voice, and open the door, I will come in to him, and will sup with him, and he with me" (Revelation 3:20).

Isn't it wonderful to have some famous or great person come into your home, even if it is only for a single meal? Have you ever entertained the mayor, a judge, one of our legislators, the governor, or a senator in your home? If you have, how proud and inspired you must have been at the presence of such a person. You were probably thrilled as you listened eagerly to every word he spoke. When you told your friends about your famous guest, you no doubt quoted some of the things that he said. It was an event that will always be one of the high lights in your life, and you will always remember it.

Knocking at your door is one who is greater than any great man. He is the King of kings. How proud you should be to open the door to Him. How eagerly you ought to listen as He speaks to you, and how anxiously you ought to repeat what He says. The best part is that Jesus is available as a constant guest. Won't you invite Him in daily and take time to know Him better? His presence will be an eternal blessing to you and your house.

The Devil's Playground

It was Frank Van Valin who said, "The devil's playground is a mental vacuum which is impoverished from lack of truth. You could never tempt a satisfied man with garbage, but the prodigal was hungry, and would have eaten tough, fibrous corn husks. A mind that is not saturated with truth is a vulnerable prey, and can be tempted with Satan's husks. The devil's most fertile field of operation is made up of impoverished minds."

The idlers are the ones who get into trouble. This is true whether they live in the slums or in palatial homes. The human mind is so constituted that it abhors a vacuum. Jesus told a story one day of a house that was occupied by an evil spirit, but the evil spirit was evicted and the house was swept clean. No one moved in, however, and soon the evil spirit came back with seven others, and the last state was worse than the first.

Our lives are like that. If we become Christians and sweep the dirt from our lives but do not fill them with Christian activities, we soon shall be a lot worse off than we were in the beginning.

Many people do not realize that we cannot serve both God and Satan. If the mind is filled with good things, there will be no place for evil ones. Samson got into trouble because he crossed over into Philistine territory and associated with evil companions. If he had been at home with good friends, he would not have been tempted to do wrong. David would not have blasted his own good name if he had turned his thoughts from an indiscreet girl to the starry heavens, and repeated: "The heavens declare the glory of God; and the firmament sheweth his handiwork."

The secret, then, is to change the subject when evil thoughts or desires come to you. The devil cannot come into your life unless you open the door to him. "Resist the devil, and he will flee from you," said James.

He Who Loves Silver

A long time ago King Solomon said, "He that loveth silver shall not be satisfied with silver; nor he that loveth abundance with increase" (Ecclesiastes 5:10).

How true that is! When a person reaches his goal of saving one hundred dollars, he finds that, instead of being satisfied, he now wants five hundred dollars. When he reaches five hundred, nothing less than one thousand will do, and then ten thousand, and on and on. We hear a lot about a disease called arteriosclerosis these days. But did you ever hear of "materiosclerosis"? A doctor says that it is one of the major killers of our time. "It is a frequent medical syndrome," he says, "a man killing himself in the mad, materialistic race of trying to be the richest man in the cemetery." Is that the purpose of life? Is that all young people have ahead of them? Is there no greater goal than the accumulation of *things?*

Possessions reveal a lot about a person—whether he is wise or foolish, humble or vain, refined or coarse, righteous or wicked. The kind of books and magazines you have tells much about the kind of person you are. The kind of pictures you have on the walls of your room, the kind of souvenirs you collect, and the sort of drinks you have in the refrigerator— all these things tell a story about you.

Perhaps clothes are your chief interest. Are you going through life like a flitting butterfly, forgetful of the fact that the winter is coming? You are going to have to leave all of your possessions behind when you come to the end of life. Seek a more worthy goal than the accumulation of things.

"Lay not up for yourselves treasures upon earth, where moth and rust doth corrupt, and where thieves break through and steal: but lay up for yourself treasures in heaven, . . . for where your treasure is, there will your heart be also" (Matthew 6: 19-21).

Help Yourself to Happiness

Everyone wants to be happy, but there are few who realize how to attain real happiness. Many young people are in a hurry to get married. "If only I could get married, all my problems would be solved and I would really be happy," seems to be the sentiment. To be sure, marriage can bring happiness, but it isn't a guarantee of it. Some of the most miserable people in the world are that way because of a hasty or foolish marriage. Millions of people are trying to get out of their marriages. They have found that real life is a lot different from what is portrayed in books, on television, or on the silver screen. Marriage carries a lot of responsibilities with it, many of which often are not pleasant.

"Give me money and a big car, and I'll be supremely happy," declares a young man. But there are countless numbers of rich playboys who have found that their millions didn't bring happiness. They flit from one indulgence to another, trying to find something to break the dull monotony of their lives. But happiness seems always to elude them.

"Give me fame and I'll not ask for anything else," says some ambitious girl. "Let me have beautiful clothing, my name in lights, and the applause of the multitudes, and I'll be in the height of glory." There are thousands who have had all those things. At first the glamor was exhilarating, but when the newness wore off, and the job resolved itself into plain, hard work, happiness began to fade. It is important to remember that there are hundreds of stars who have beauty, money, and fame, but many of them are the most unhappy people to be found in the world. What is wrong when people cannot find happiness? Why does it seem to elude so many of them?

Happiness is not something that can be bought; it is the by-product of a duty performed well. If you want to be happy, forget yourself and think of others. Help some young child to make a toy and see the joy come into his face. Be a friend to some neglected young person in school, and experience the gratitude he has for you. Do some chores around the home without your parents having to prod you, and see how much more they appreciate you. Volunteer to be of service to the church, and learn the satisfaction of feeling that God is pleased. Help a poor person who cannot repay the favor that you do for him. It will make you happy.

John Jacob Astor, grandson of the man who started the Astor fortune in the fur business, came to be worth two hundred million dollars. Did he and his wife find happiness in merely having money? No. They found happiness through giving away money as good stewards of God and serving the church of which they were members. His wife often went incognito among the poor, helping them in many ways. The poor knew this rich woman only as "Sister Augusta."

There is a joy that comes from accomplishment. To have the most beautiful flower garden in the neighborhood, to make an attractive table during your manual training hour, to write an exceptional story for your school paper, to be a football hero, to have your boss say at the end of the summer, "We've never had anyone who did a better job than you, and we want you again next summer"—these things will bring a great deal of joy and happiness. The greatest happiness will come to you if you love God and keep His commandments. Such love and obedience will bring you lasting joy and peace. So, help yourself to happiness!

Can You Keep a Secret?

Have you ever overheard two young persons talking something like this? "Please tell me all about it," begs one of them. "I promise not to tell a soul." "But I promised not to tell," replies the second one. "I cross my heart I won't pass it on," vows the first one. "All right, but this is absolutely confidential." So the secret is whispered into the ear of the other, and once more gossip is on its way.

It was Solomon who said long ago, "A talebearer revealeth secrets: but he that is of a faithful spirit concealeth the matter" (Proverbs 11:13), and later, "He that goeth about as a tablebearer revealeth secrets: therefore meddle not with him that flattereth with his lips" (Proverbs 20:19). Perhaps you have heard the story of a man who was being pestered by another to give him certain information. "Can you keep a secret?" he asked. "Yes!" assured the one who was pressuring him. "Well, I can too," he said, and refused to give it.

Secrets can be terrible things, and you ought never to ask anyone to share them with you. Curiosity is strong, and you may be very eager to know certain things, but unless you have a very strong will, you will never be able to keep what you have learned to yourself. Sooner or later you will be tempted to tell the secret. Maybe you will tell only one person; that person will tell only one person, but the story will soon be out.

There is an old Greek legend that Apollo challenged Pan to a contest on the flute. King Midas, who was the judge, gave the prize to Pan, a favorite of his, although his playing was inferior to that of Apollo. This angered Apollo, and he determined to show his contempt for his dishonest judge by causing the ears of an ass to grow on King Midas' head. The king, in great dismay, fled to his apartment and sent in haste for a barber to fashion a wig that would cover his ugly ears. The barber was sworn to secrecy, but after a while the maintaining of silence seemed unbearable. So the barber dug a hole and shouted the secret into the hole. Time passed, and reeds grew over the hole. The reeds heard the secret of the king and passed it on. It was not long before everyone knew and were talking about what had happened to King Midas.

If you tell a secret, you will have broken a promise, told a lie, and shattered someone's faith in you. You will have blackened your own reputation so that no one will ever want to confide in you again. Worse yet, a lie is a sin, and unless you sincerely repent and ask forgiveness of God, you will not be saved.

If you tell a secret someone may be hurt, be made ashamed or embarrassed, or even lose a good reputation. Some years ago a woman died who had not spoken a word for many years. She had passed on some gossip about a young girl, and this had caused the girl to take her own life. The woman resolved that never again would her tongue get anyone into trouble. We need not go to the extreme of not talking at all. We need only to refrain from talking about things that have been told to us in confidence.

Of course some secrets may not necessarily be bad in themselves, and yet the time may not be right for telling them. You must not be guilty of passing on even good news when you have promised not to do so. You will be depriving those who are chiefly concerned with the news the joy of making it known to others. Although others may be thrilled to hear what you have to say, they will never think as much of you because you have broken faith with those who trusted you. Do not ask for secrets to be told to you, and you will not be guilty of revealing them. If secrets are told to you, be very careful to keep them safely locked in a corner of your mind.

Messages From the Dead

When we consider messages from the dead, we are not talking about a medium, or fortune-teller, who claims to bring word from the spirit world. Such people are mere fakes. Indeed, God put a death penalty on them in ancient times, so that there would be no confusing their false messages with the revelations He gave through the prophets. Nevertheless, the book of Hebrews speaks of the faithfulness of Abel and God's acceptance of his gift, and we read, "By it he being dead yet speaketh" (Hebrews 11:4).

You know the story of Eve and her temptation. Her message to you probably would be, "Don't ever believe anything the devil tells you. I trusted him, and was deceived."

Noah's family was saved because of their faith and obedience. Noah would probably say, "Trust in God and He'll save you, too."

One day Abraham was put to a severe test by God. He was asked to sacrifice his son on the altar. Abraham was horrified, but he was so sure of God that he obeyed. He was ready to slay the boy when an angel stopped him and showed him how a ram had been provided as a substitute. We can hear Abraham saying to us, "I trusted God, and He didn't fail me. You must trust in Him too."

Jacob was a shrewd young fellow who thought he could outwit others. He deceived his brother, and his father, and his Uncle Laban. But his Uncle Laban also outwitted him. Only unhappiness and a spoiled family life came as the result. Jacob's message from the dead would no doubt be, "Play it fair; don't ever try to deceive anyone."

Read your Bible to see how many other "messages from the dead" you can find. There are many. Some will warn you against falling into certain sins. Others will help you to strengthen your faith in God. Be sure to heed these messages.

The "Theses" that Shook the World

For several hundred years after it was founded, the church held fairly close to the teachings of Jesus. Then little by little there came changes. There was a struggle for power, which brought forth a hierarchy, with its bishops, archbishops, cardinals, and finally a pope who claimed power over the whole world. Doctrine also underwent changes. Extra-Biblical doctrines and practices were brought in, such as the worship of Mary and the saints, purgatory, absolution, the confessional, priesthood, reciting of the rosary, indulgences, sign of the cross, etc. From time to time courageous leaders raised their voices in protest, but they were persecuted and some of them burned at the stake. Soldiers were used to destroy whole movements in several instances, and the Catholic Church held control of a large portion of the world from about A.D. 500 to 1500. Kings were forced to acknowledge the supremacy of the pope, or be excommunicated.

In 1517, John Tetzel came into Germany selling indulgences as an agent of the pope. These indulgences were pieces of paper which the people could buy to have their sins forgiven (even sins they had not committed, but planned to commit), or to get their relatives out of purgatory. The people were foolish enough to believe that their sins could be forgiven in such a way, so they provided much money for the pope by buying the indulgences.

There was a young monk by the name of Martin Luther who was amazed to find a lot of things in the Bible which the priests did not have in the breviary. He realized how far the Catholic Church had departed from the simple practices of the New Testament church and felt that these practices should be restored. Among other things, Tetzel's sales trip made Luther highly indignant. He was determined to challenge the false teachings of the church. So he wrote out ninety-five theses which he offered to debate with anyone, and posted them in the accustomed place on the door of the church at Wittenberg. He had no idea what the result would be, but in a short time all of Europe was ablaze with the news that Luther had defied the pope. He was ordered to go to Rome and give account of himself, but he refused to do so and was excommunicated. He burned his excommunication paper on the campus of the university where he taught. Many people agreed with Luther's beliefs, but the emperor brought him to trial, where he took his historic stand. He refused to withdraw anything he had said, so was declared an outlaw. To save his life some friends took him to the castle of Wartburg where he translated the Bible into German. He believed that the German people should be able to read the Bible in their own language. In the course of time, followings grew up around certain great leaders like Luther, and these crystallized into the Protestant denominations.

There are several great principles of Protestantism with which we ought to be familiar: 1. the authority of the Scriptures; 2. the right of every man to read the Bible and to understand it for himself; 3. salvation by faith in Christ and obedience to His commands; 4. the right for worshipers to go directly to God through Christ in prayer rather than through Mary, a priest, or saints.

Martin Luther took a big step toward restoring the church to its original state. Needless to say, we do not want to follow the practices of a church such as Martin Luther knew. Nor do we want to follow man-made practices that have arisen in many denominational churches. Let us be certain that we look to the Scriptures as our sole authority of faith and practice.

The Kingdom in Your Heart

One day the Pharisees came to Jesus and wanted to know when the kingdom of God should come. Jesus replied, "Behold, the kingdom of God is within you" (Luke 17:21). Jesus is the king who will rule over your life when you become a citizen of His kingdom by being born spiritually (John 3:5) at the time of your baptism.

Let's take a look at the kingdom in your heart. In this kingdom you are the *mayor*. It is your business to know and administer the laws of Christ, all of which are designed to develop you as a Christian and provide for your welfare.

You are also going to be the *policeman*. If you have a policeman in your inner life, you will not have to worry about one in uniform on the outside. This policeman will probably be kept very busy, but he will keep you out of trouble if you will follow his advice. As policeman, what are you going to do about that thief in your life who is ready to steal? Maybe that thief wants to steal good grades through cheating; someone's good name, through lying; or someone's good character through tempting him to sin. What are you going to do about the law-breaker, who decides to break the speed limits, disregard stop signs, and run red lights?

You also are to be the *judge,* and if you do violate the laws of God, you will be brought before your conscience for acquittal or condemnation. It will not let you off easy; indeed, it will keep you perfectly wretched until you have repented and been forgiven. Even then, the remembrance of the sin will be with you for a long time.

In this kingdom you are going to be the *truant officer*. If you are tempted to skip school, he will be right after you, reminding you how important it is to get an education. If you are tempted to miss church services, he will remind you how important and rewarding it is to worship and serve God. He will help you to remember that gathering together with other Christians to worship God is essential for the well-being of your soul. Soon the truant officer will have you so much in the habit of attending church services that you will never want to miss. You will love spending time in the worship of God in His house.

You will also be the *fireman* in the kingdom, putting out all unholy desires before they destroy you. This will be far more important than putting out the fire in a burning building. A building can be rebuilt, but a burnt-out life seldom can be replaced.

You will be the *builder* of a home in your kingdom. Will you put into it cheap materials and poor workmanship? It is up to you to choose. Every day you are selecting some kind of building material for your life and are arranging it as you go. Are you following the blueprint given in the Bible, or are you trying to build without a plan, only to have your life destroyed by a wind of circumstance or temptation some time in the future? Character is pretty strongly shaped by the time you are out of your teens, so these years of building are tremendously important. It is very difficult for people to change when they become adults, for by this time they are fairly well set in their ways. Will your house of life be able to stand the storms when they come?

Surprising as it may seem, you are also the *garbage collector* in your kingdom. You are going to collect all of the dirt and trash that comes into your life and promptly dispose of it before it brings sickness to your soul. Evil thoughts, desires, suggestions, and other things will come to you from every side. Get rid of them as soon as possible.

Christ is the supreme ruler of your kingdom, but it is up to you to keep your kingdom in good condition so He can rule it. Keep your heart and life fit for eternal life with God in heaven!

Can Every Man Be Bought?

In these days when dishonesty, theft, and embezzlement seem to be so prevalent, it might seem as if every man does have his price. Perhaps we feel that every person can be bought if the price is high enough to suit him. There have always been people who had such a love and yearning for gold that they would go to any extent to possess it.

In the early days of Rome, when that city was at war with the Sabines, Tarpeia, daughter of the keeper of the citadel, agreed to open the gates for the enemy if the soldiers would give her what they had on their left arms. They agreed, but instead of giving her their golden bracelets, they cast on her their shields until she was crushed. This is one example of how foolish it is to sell one's self for any price.

During the days of the judges, Delilah was loved by the strong man, Samson. But Delilah loved money. Approached by some Philistine nobles who each offered her eleven hundred pieces of silver for the knowledge, she learned from Samson the secret of his strength. This began a series of incidents that led to Samson's death.

In our own American history, when Major Andre was captured as a spy by three Revolutionary soldiers, he offered them a lot of money if they would let him go free. Even though they were in great need, they refused to listen to him, and delivered him to their superior officers. They were men without a price. They could not be bought for any price.

It is true that Judas has his price and sold his soul for thirty pieces of silver. But there were eleven other disciples who did not. Those men could easily have sold out, but they loved Jesus and valued their own souls more than any amount of wealth. Most of them died a martyr's death. Perhaps they remembered the temptation of Jesus, and how Satan offered Him every inducement to take the easy road and worship

Satan. But Jesus did not yield to any of Satan's temptations.

There is no amount of gold or silver that is as valuable as a human soul. If you sell yourself to Satan, you will be getting the worst end of the bargain. Jesus could not be bought; eleven of the twelve apostles could not be bought; many men and women today cannot be bought by Satan at any price. We hope you are one of these. Many times the glitter of great wealth attained by dishonest means will dazzle you. But just remember, your soul is worth much more than material things, for it will last forever—long after the things of this world have passed away.

Right or Wrong?

Life is becoming increasingly complex, is it not? It seems that problems are always arising to worry us. That is particularly true of things having to do with right or wrong. We become puzzled, and we do not know what to do. We are pressed for an immediate decision, and are not at all sure what course a Christian should take. If things were only black or white, perhaps it would be easy to know. But in many cases they are gray—a mixture of good and evil. We feel that we ought to reject the evil, but some good is there, and so the devil whispers that surely that makes it all right. How are we going to decide? How are we going to choose so that our consciences won't keep bothering us?

There is an old fable about a blind man who used to be able to tell the identity of any animal that was placed in his hands. On one occasion someone brought him a baby wolf. He felt it all over, and then said doubtfully, "I do not know whether thy father was a dog or a wolf; but this I know, that I would not trust thee among a flock of sheep." That is a good example for us today. When in doubt, *don't!*

Now let us take a look at some of our problems. Is it right to tell a lie? Oh, we all know it is wrong to tell a big lie, but what about a little "white" one? Surely there cannot be anything wrong with that. At least that is what a lot of people think. But God has not divided lies into two categories—white and black, small and large. To God a lie is a lie, and lying is a sin. We read in the Bible that liars will not enter the kingdom of heaven. So, is it wrong to lie?

Is it right to take a drink when you are with people who are drinking? Perhaps you don't plan to make drinking a habit, but you want these people to approve of you. They want to feel that you are as weak as they are. You know the devastating, habit-forming effects of alcohol. You know the bad example you are setting. Can you afford, as a Christian, to compromise your high standards? Will your friends really respect you for it?

If it is wrong to lie even occasionally, and take a drink occasionally, is it wrong to be immoral just once in a while, when you are with that kind of crowd? Where are you going to draw the line? Please remember that any type of immorality is sin. We must account for all our sins.

Is it all right to watch a television show that is unwholesome, or should it be turned off? Is it right to read a book that is not decent? What effect might it have on you?

Here are some tests to help you make the correct decision as to whether something is right or wrong:

1. Will God approve? If He will not, you dare not do it.

2. Is it good for the body, mind, and spirit, or are there dangers connected with it—dangers that will harm your soul?

3. Does it lift up the soul, or does it have a degrading effect? Will it build honor and self-respect, or tend to tear them down?

4. If everyone were doing it, would the world be better or worse? Might it bring some regrets?

5. Can you ask the Lord to bless you in doing it? Do you feel that Jesus would be willing to participate if He were here?

Remember these five guides for making decisions. Answer them honestly. Then ask God's help as you choose between right and wrong each day of your life.

The "Rock" of the Pilgrims

When the Pilgrims landed in Massachusetts, December 21, 1620, to establish a colony in the new world, they brought along with them a "Rock." It was not Plymouth Rock, although they landed near that famous boulder. They brought along Christ, "the rock of our salvation."

These young people (for they were young people, thirty-nine of them being under twenty-one, and only eleven of them being as old as forty) had not come to America to go native and to live by the law of the jungle. Before they ever left the "Mayflower" they drew up the "Mayflower Compact," in which they stated that their journey had been undertaken for "the glory of God and the advancement of the Christian faith." They had been God-fearing people before the ship sailed; they continued to be God-fearing after they arrived.

Soon they erected a meeting house where services were held. They fortified the roof with six cannons that they had brought along. Each Sunday they assembled at the beat of a drum and marched to the church building, carrying their muskets with them. God was real to them, and for the sake of serving Him according to the dictates of their consciences, they had left the homeland. Now, at the risk of their lives they were being faithful to Him in the midst of danger.

These were the people who brought Christ to New England, and made religion a vital part of the life of America. There was a period of nine years when they had no minister, but the church did not fail, nor did the Pilgrims forget God. Sickness played havoc with them during that first hard, cold winter. More than half of them died. But they did not harden their hearts nor turn against God. They remained faithful to Him, trusting that He would take care of them if they were striving to do His will. The following fall, after the crops were harvested, they celebrated the first Thanksgiving Day in

America, thanking God for His mercies and His goodness.

We can learn a valuable lesson from the Pilgrims. No matter what we do or where we go, if we take Christ, "the rock of our salvation," with us, our lives will be more successful. Even during difficult times Christ will be with us and will help us if we let Him. Don't blame God if troubles come to you. Examine yourself to see if you are being as faithful to Him as you should be. Then trust Him explicitly that He will see you through your troubles. Carry Christ, the "Rock," with you all your life—the same "Rock" that the Pilgrims brought with them to the new world.

Is the Bible True?

There are many religions in the world, and many sacred books, but Christians look upon the Bible as the one and only written revelation of God. It alone expresses His love and divine will for men. It is a book of history, biography, poetry, prophecy, and revelation. How can we be sure that the Bible is true and that it actually was given by God?

1. The teachings of the Bible, when put to the test, are found to be true. No other teachings have ever surpassed Jesus' teachings. Jesus said, "If any man will do his [God's] will, he shall know of the doctrine, whether it be of God" (John 7:17).

2. The Bible offers things no pagan religion offers—the love of God, and the Saviour of the world. It transforms and uplifts the life, making new creatures of men no matter how sinful they have been. It gives meaning to life, offers salvation, and gives to men the hope of a life beyond. So sure were the disciples of the divinity of Jesus and the miracles He performed that they were willing to die for their faith.

3. Although the books of the Bible were written over a period of fifteen hundred years, and by forty or more writers, there is one theme that runs from Genesis to Revelation: God's plan for redeeming men, all of whom need redemption.

4. The books of the Bible were collected by men who were in a position to know of their authenticity, both in Old and New Testament times. The apocryphal books were rejected by the Jews as being noninspired. Jesus never once quoted from them. They are books of history and contain no divine revelation, not having been written by divinely inspired men.

5. Archaeology verifies Biblical writings. In Bible lands there are cities that have been buried by the sands of the desert for many centuries, and in some cases before the first books of the Bible were ever written. Upon being unearthed,

these cities are proving that certain statements in the Bible are true. The Holy Spirit directed the writing, and we can rely upon it.

6. The writings of the enemies of the church prove that various books were in existence at the time of the writings and accepted as divinely inspired. Efforts have been made many times to destroy the Bible. But God will not allow His Word to be destroyed.

7. During the first three centuries there were many quotations from the books of the Bible. These have come to us. Even though we don't have any first-century originals, we know the writings were in existence. The quotations correspond with what we have in our Bibles.

8. When all of the early manuscripts are laid side by side, together with the separate portions of quotations and the translations that have been made in many different languages, it is found that we have the same message in all of them. Scribes occasionally misspelled words or omitted some; but by comparing the manuscripts with others corrections were made; so we may be sure that we have a reliable translation of the Bible today. We have the message that was started on its way so long ago, under the guidance of the Holy Spirit.

9. When the Dead Sea scrolls were discovered, one of them contained a copy of the book of Isaiah, dating about 150 B.C. This is one thousand years older than any other copy we have. This copy, when compared with the one in our Bibles, proves how accurately the scribes transmitted the Scriptures from century to century.

10. While no complete Bible has been found that was dated earlier than A.D. 350, Bible manuscripts are closer in time to the originals than are any other ancient writings. Between Sophocles and the earliest manuscript of his plays there is a space of fourteen hundred years; Euripides, sixteen hundred years; Plato, thirteen hundred years.

Your Brother's Keeper

The origin of this topic goes back almost to the beginning of time, when Cain killed Abel, his brother, and God called him to account. "Am I my brother's keeper?" asked Cain when God demanded to know the whereabouts of Abel. God let Cain know that he did have a responsibility for the welfare of his brother. We have that same responsibility today.

1. We have a responsibility for the *physical health* of others. If you find that you have a contagious disease, such as the flu, stay home and go to bed rather than go where others are and expose them. Maybe you have been looking forward to a big event at the church or school, but if you go you may cause other people to become sick. Even if you have only a cold, you can transfer germs that will do damage. If it is absolutely necessary for you to go somewhere, stay as far away from others as possible.

2. You are your brother's keeper *mentally*. If you are more intelligent than others, help those who do not make as good grades as you. Perhaps there are good reasons for their not doing as well as you. Under better circumstances perhaps they would surprise you. Thomas Aquinas was considered a dullard by his classmates, but he became one of the greatest scholars during the Middle Ages. Thomas Edison was looked upon as "addled," but he has blessed the whole world with his inventions.

Help your friends to solve their problems if you are the capable one. They will always appreciate you. Give good advice, if you have wisdom, and help others to avoid some of the pitfalls that ruin lives.

3. You are your brother's keeper *spiritually*. Ministers, missionaries, Bible college professors, etc., feel this keenly. But very often, the average person does not. Dr. Albert L. Shelton, missionary to Tibet, had been held by Chinese bandits for

some time, and only narrowly missed death. He returned to America to recuperate. His friends begged him not to go back to Tibet, but because the Dalai Lama had invited him, the first missionary, to enter the forbidden city of Lhasa, he felt he must return. Dr. Shelton knew that he was his brother's keeper.

You can be your brother's keeper wherever you are. Set a good example for others, and help them to walk in right paths. As far as you can, keep them from associating with bad companions, and from going to bad places. Invite them to come with you to church where they will meet young people who will not be a source of temptation to them. Show them how they can have fun without having to resort to dancing and drinking. Help them to fill their lives with good things so that there will be no time or desire for evil things.

Discuss Christianity with your friends, and help them with their spiritual problems. Reassure the doubtful ones as best you can and build up faith within them. Be constructive, and show them that Christianity is a happier, more satisfying way of life than any other. Help them to see that God wants to lead them into true happiness and service. Win them to Christ, so that they may share with you the blessed life which is ahead. Yes, you are your brother's keeper, so begin now to live up to this great responsibility!

Whose Child Was Jesus?

The Christmas season, with its beautiful stories of the birth of Jesus and the colorful nativity pageants, points out the fact of the virgin birth of Jesus. Yet many modern scholars are constantly attacking that truth. Why do they try to deny that Jesus is God's Son, born of a virgin? Let us see what is involved in the matter.

Those who attack the virgin birth usually claim one of two things: 1. That Jesus was the natural son of Joseph and Mary; 2. That Jesus was the illegitimate son of Mary. The first claim would completely falsify the Scriptures, for Jesus could not possibly be our Saviour if both of His parents were human. He would have been but a weak sinner himself, just like other people, and could not have made atonement for us. Furthermore, the story of Joseph shows that the coming child was not his. He was about to put Mary away privately, but the angel explained that the child had been begotten of the Holy Spirit and was to be the promised Messiah. The second claim is even more ridiculous than the first. If Jesus were simply an illegitimate child, then Mary was a weak girl who yielded to temptation, instead of being "the handmaid of the Lord," chosen to be the mother of the Messiah. Again, it would mean that we have no Saviour and are yet in our sins. We would have no assurance of forgiveness or the promise of everlasting life.

The virgin birth is no problem for those who believe in God and His power as the Creator of the universe. Of course the virgin birth was a miracle, and miracles are a problem for some people. But God, who was mighty enough to create a world like this, and who created man complete in the first place, surely was able to give life to an invisible cell that grew into the body of the baby Jesus. Was it any more of a miracle for God to endow this single cell with life than to have created man in the beginning? These disbelieving scholars just do not like the message of Jesus, do not want to accept His authority, do not like His teachings about judgment and hell, and so try to make Him only a human being and not the divine Son of God. But trying to wish Jesus to be just a mere man does not make it so. If Jesus is not the Son of God, then the Bible cannot be trusted, God has not spoken to us, no atonement has been made, and we have no hope of everlasting life. There is a lot at stake in this matter, and the wise person will not throw away his hope of the future just because some people do not believe God's Word.

Paul said, "The times of this ignorance God winked at; but now commandeth all men every where to repent: because he hath appointed a day, in the which he will judge the world in righteousness by that man whom he hath ordained; whereof he hath given assurance unto all men, in that he hath raised him from the dead" (Acts 17:30, 31). In Hebrews 9:27, 28 we read, "And as it is appointed unto men once to die, but after this the judgment: so Christ was once offered to bear the sins of many; and unto them that look for him shall he appear the second time without sin unto salvation."

Mary knew Jesus was the Son of God. Joseph, the shepherds, the Wise-men were convinced. Simeon and Anna believed Him to be the promised Messiah. The testimony of the Scriptures and the witness to Jesus' power in His transformation of lives in the present day should be sufficient to convince us that He is the Son of God.

Finding Your Place

What a strange place this world would be if everyone did the same kind of work! Can you imagine one hundred million people in this country doing nothing but building houses or painting pictures or selling cars? Soon everyone would either starve to death or go crazy. God was wise when He placed different talents in people's lives and gave us the desire to do different things. How rich our lives are because there are thousands of different occupations from which to choose instead of just one.

Every young person faces the problem of deciding what type of work he can do best. He needs to discover what talents he has and then put them to work in the most suitable place. It is the experience of older people that no one can be truly happy and do his best until he has found work for which he is best fitted. It is up to each one of us to decide which talent he wants to develop. And preparations for using that particular talent should be made when one is young. Here are some suggestions you may wish to follow as you strive to find your place in life.

1. Do not be a wisher. That is, do not just sit down and wish that you could do something wise or great, and then forget about it. Many young people want to be successful, but they are not willing to put in the time, effort, and hard work that helps a person become successful. If a certain occupation requires years of preparation, many are content to take a less important job so they can start earning money right now. If you have the talent and desire for a certain career, start now to prepare for it. If it is a worthwhile career, many years of preparation will not be wasted.

2. Be sure that you really do have a talent or "knack" for your chosen profession. Don't select an occupation just because it seems glamorous and exciting. Even the most exciting

job can seem dull and have no appeal if a person is not suited for it.

3. Select an occupation that has some kind of lasting value. Your job should be something that will contribute to the welfare and happiness of others—one that will make the world a little bit better because you are performing your job well.

4. When you have decided upon a certain career or occupation, talk with people who are in that same career. Ask their advice as to the advantages, disadvantages, preparation, etc., connected with the job. When you have heard their advice, consider it carefully. Are you willing to make the sacrifices necessary to make a success of that certain career? After hearing the unglamorous side of the job, do you still want to try it?

5. Perhaps the most important fact to consider in selecting a lifetime work is this: Will God approve of your choice of occupation, and can you do your work to the glory of God? The Bible tells us that no matter what we do or say, we should do it to the glory of God. Pray to God that He will guide you in the very important decision of selecting an occupation. Ask Him to help you do your job to the very best of your ability. Then work hard and diligently to achieve your goal.